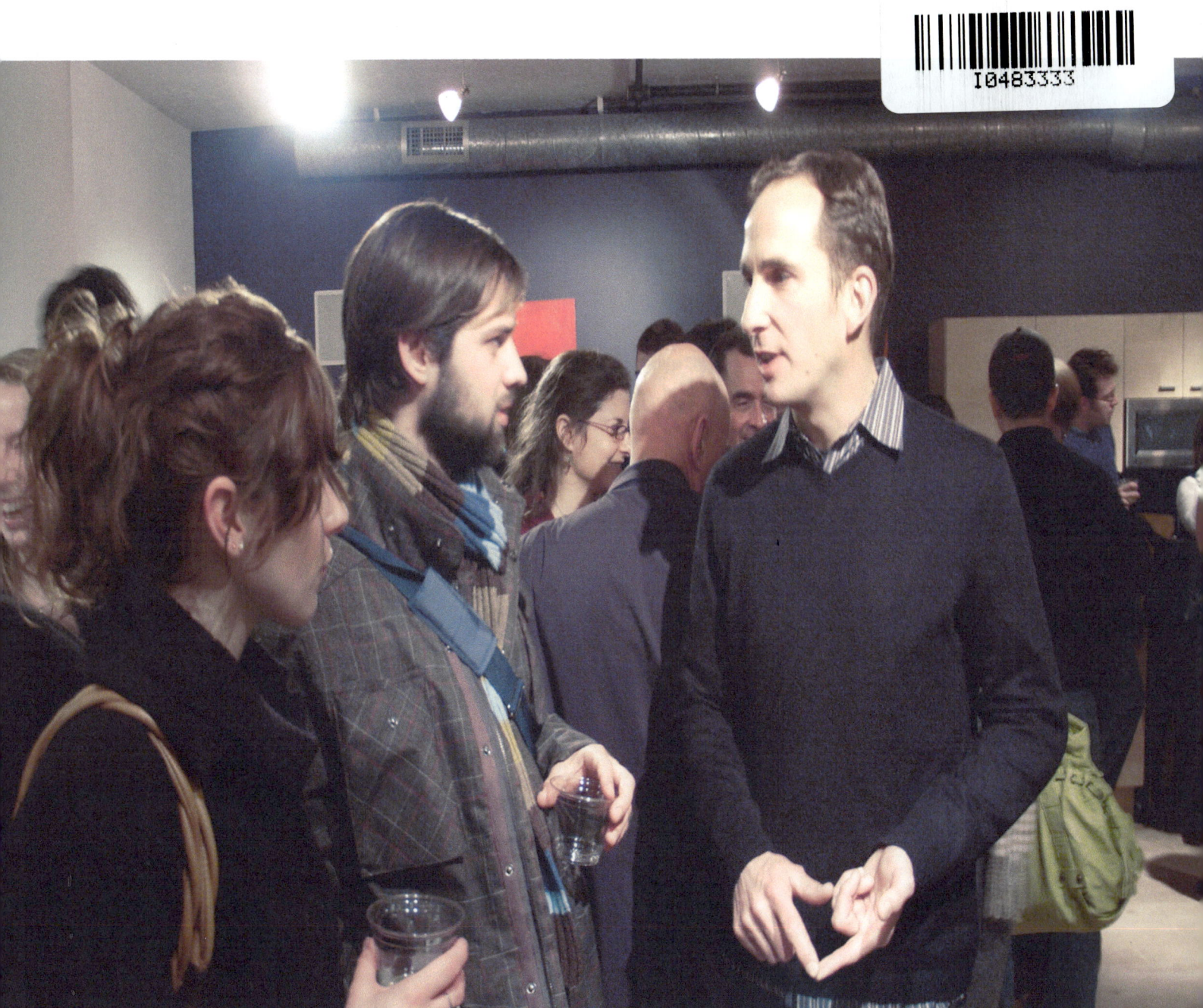

VECTOR SPACE PARADOX

[ART / PORTFOLIO / GRAPHIC NOVEL]
Copyright 2018 Daniel Stuelpnagel
All Rights Reserved.
Printed in USA
Publisher: Sequence3

ISBN 978-0-9859165-2-7

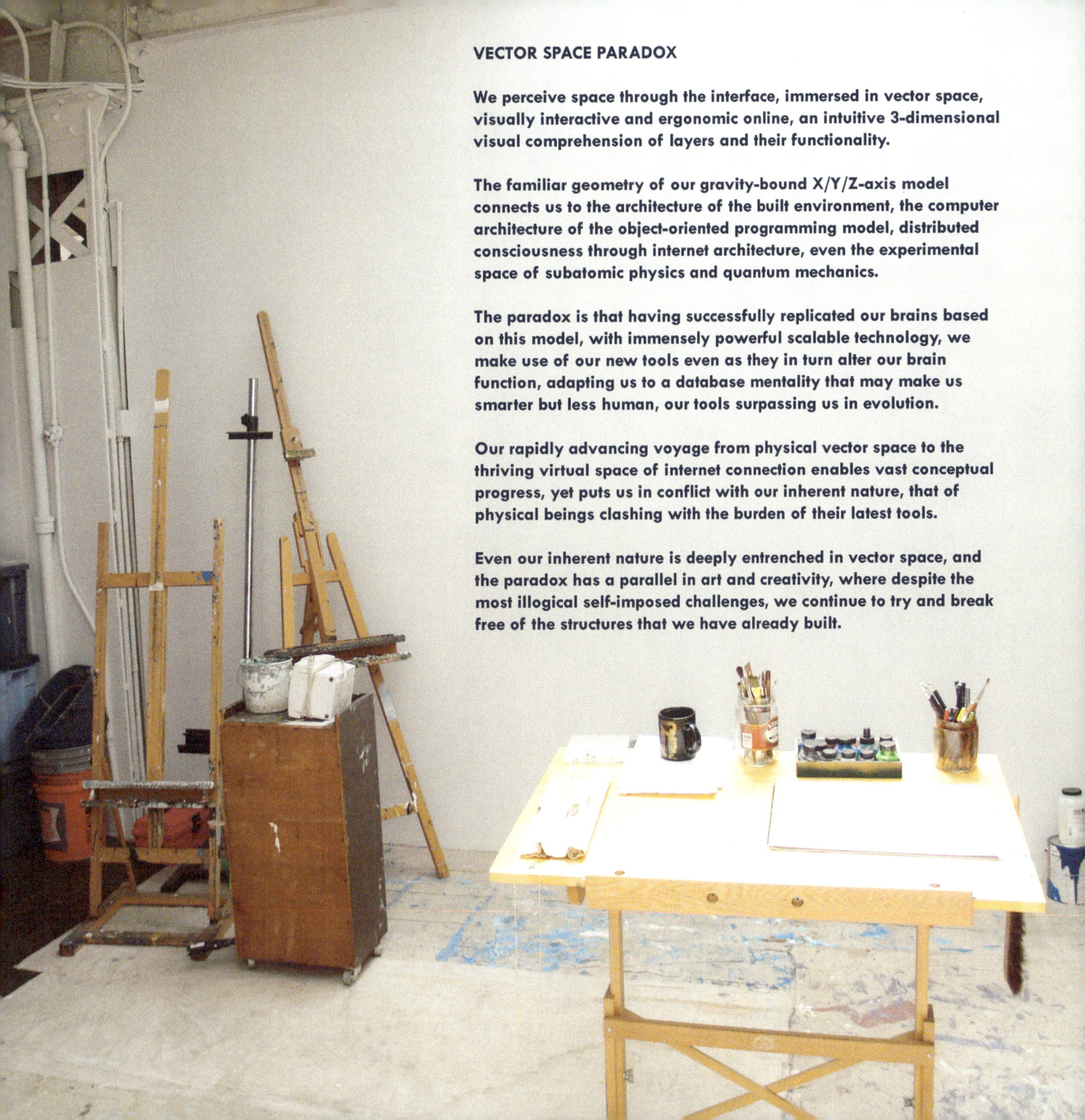

VECTOR SPACE PARADOX

We perceive space through the interface, immersed in vector space, visually interactive and ergonomic online, an intuitive 3-dimensional visual comprehension of layers and their functionality.

The familiar geometry of our gravity-bound X/Y/Z-axis model connects us to the architecture of the built environment, the computer architecture of the object-oriented programming model, distributed consciousness through internet architecture, even the experimental space of subatomic physics and quantum mechanics.

The paradox is that having successfully replicated our brains based on this model, with immensely powerful scalable technology, we make use of our new tools even as they in turn alter our brain function, adapting us to a database mentality that may make us smarter but less human, our tools surpassing us in evolution.

Our rapidly advancing voyage from physical vector space to the thriving virtual space of internet connection enables vast conceptual progress, yet puts us in conflict with our inherent nature, that of physical beings clashing with the burden of their latest tools.

Even our inherent nature is deeply entrenched in vector space, and the paradox has a parallel in art and creativity, where despite the most illogical self-imposed challenges, we continue to try and break free of the structures that we have already built.

FREEDOM
WITHIN
BOUNDARIES

2

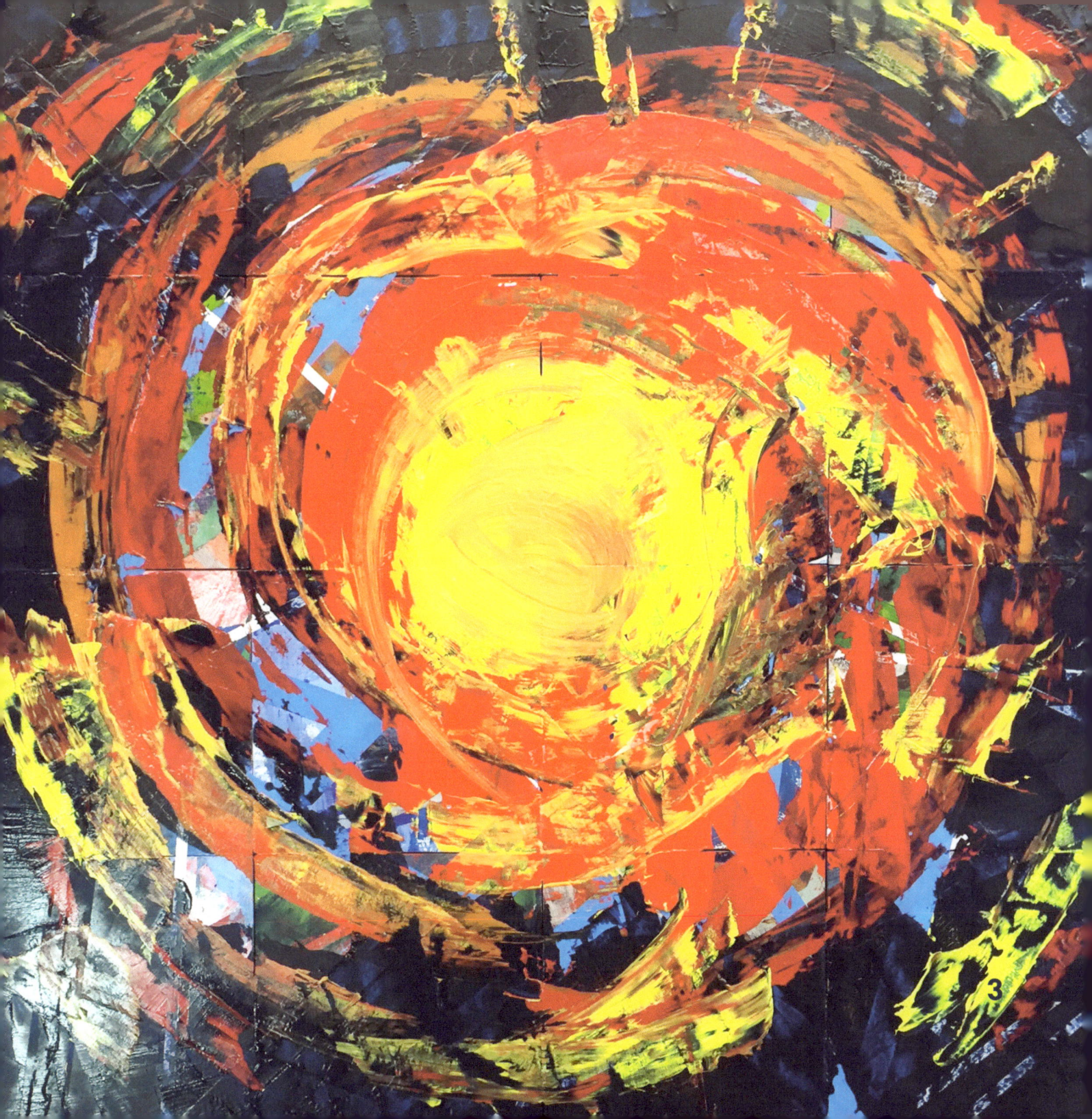

PERMUTATIONS

4

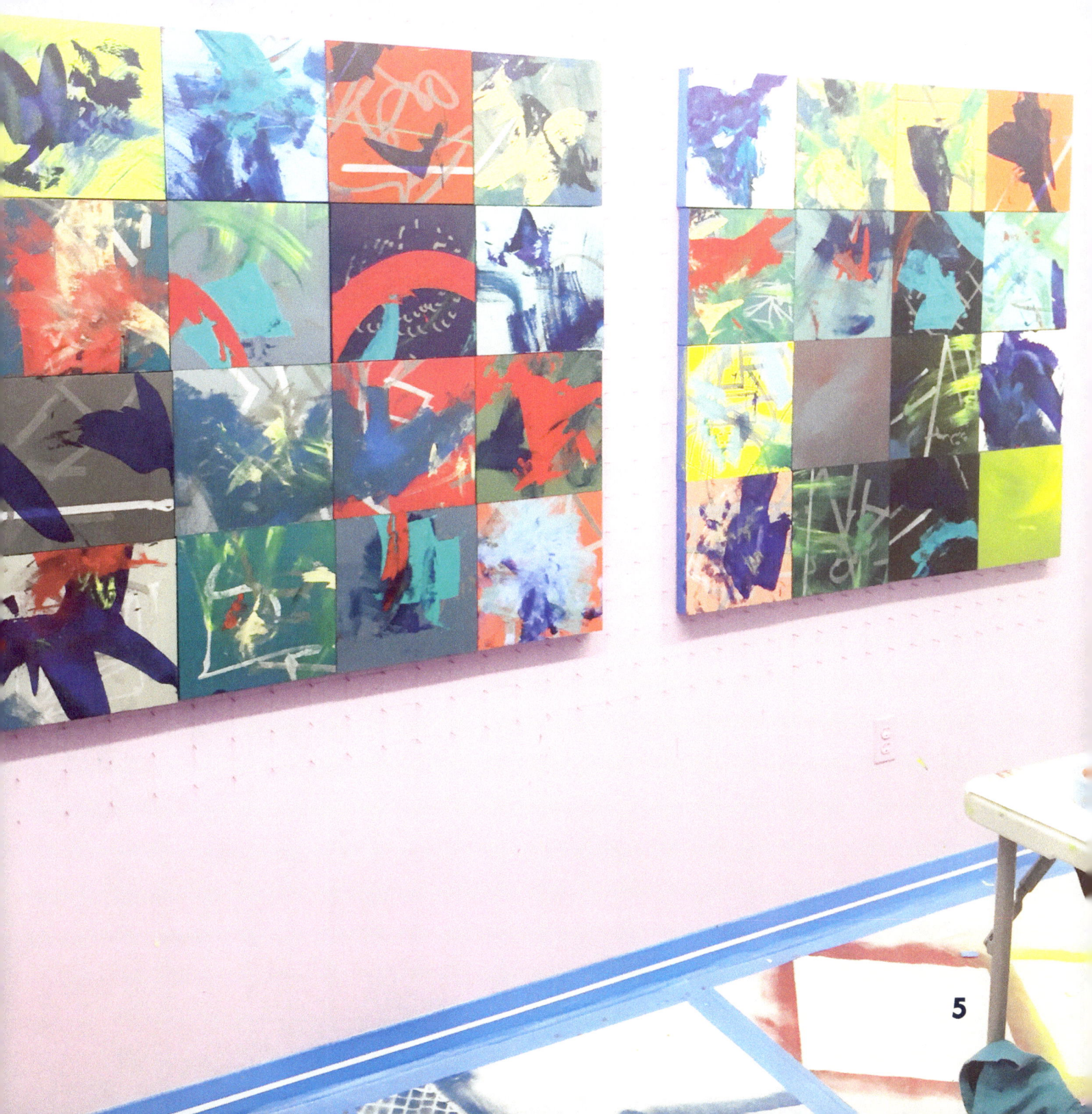

WORK IN PROGRESS

6

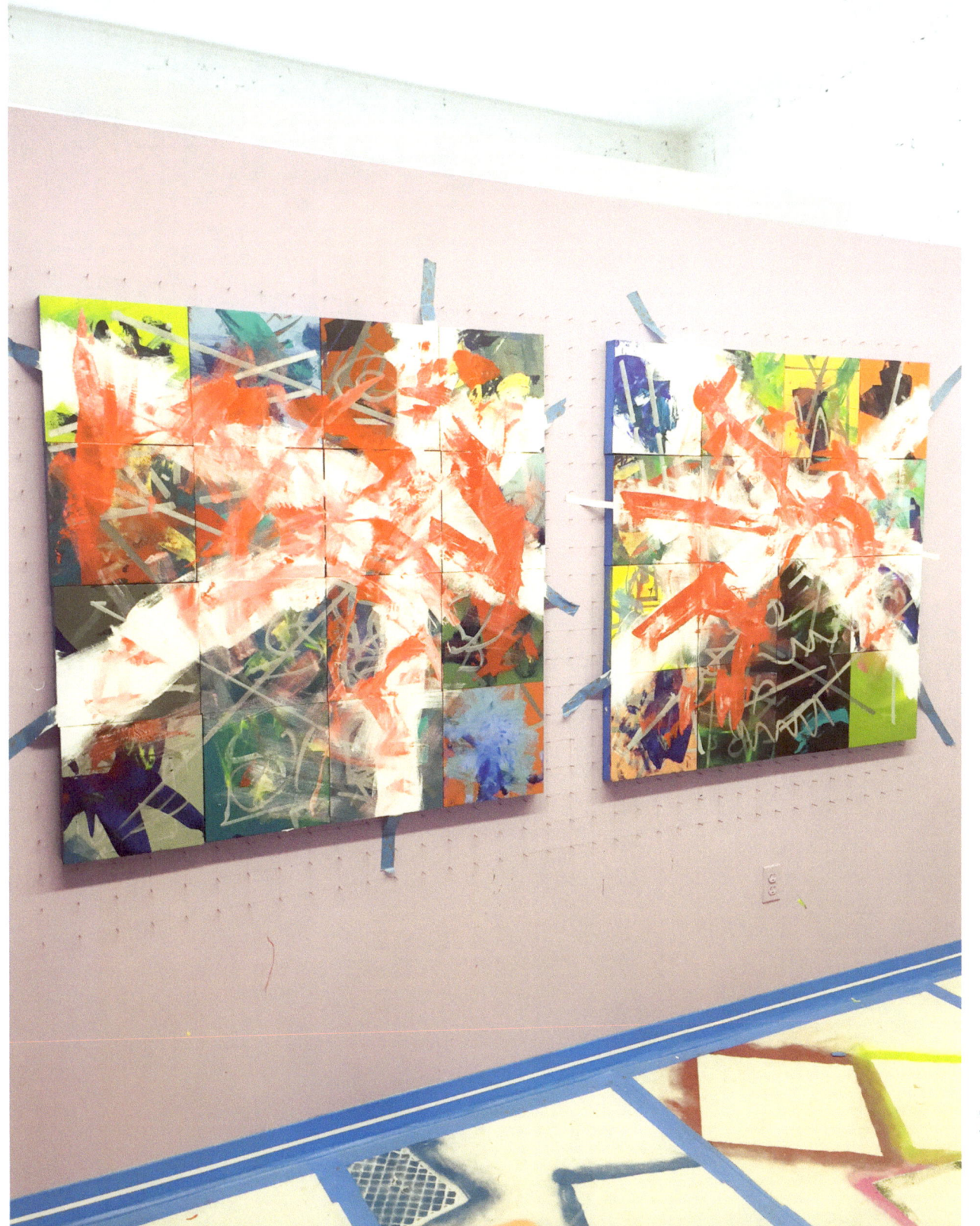

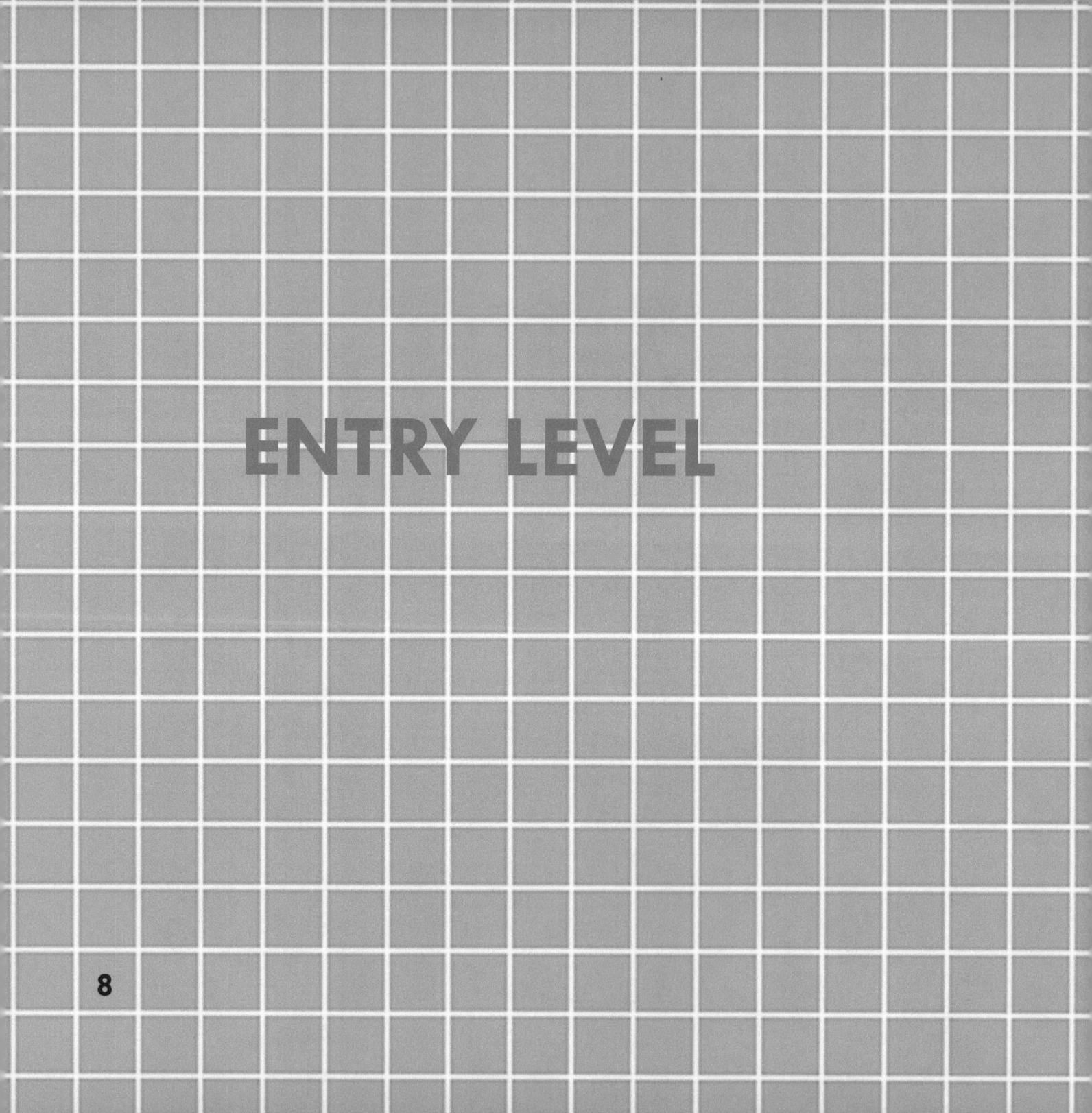

ENTRY LEVEL

8

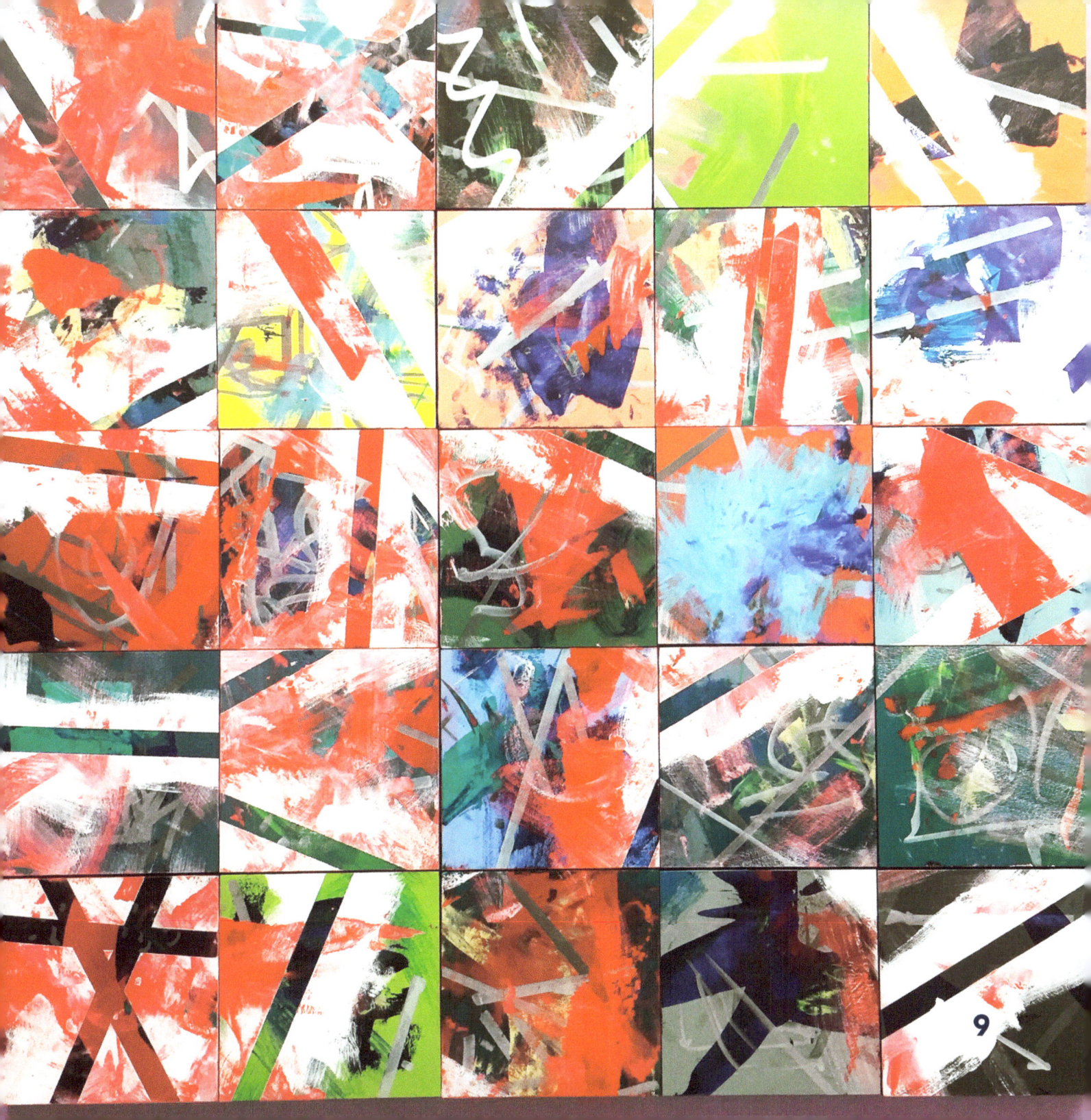

9

DIVIDE
AND
CONQUER

10

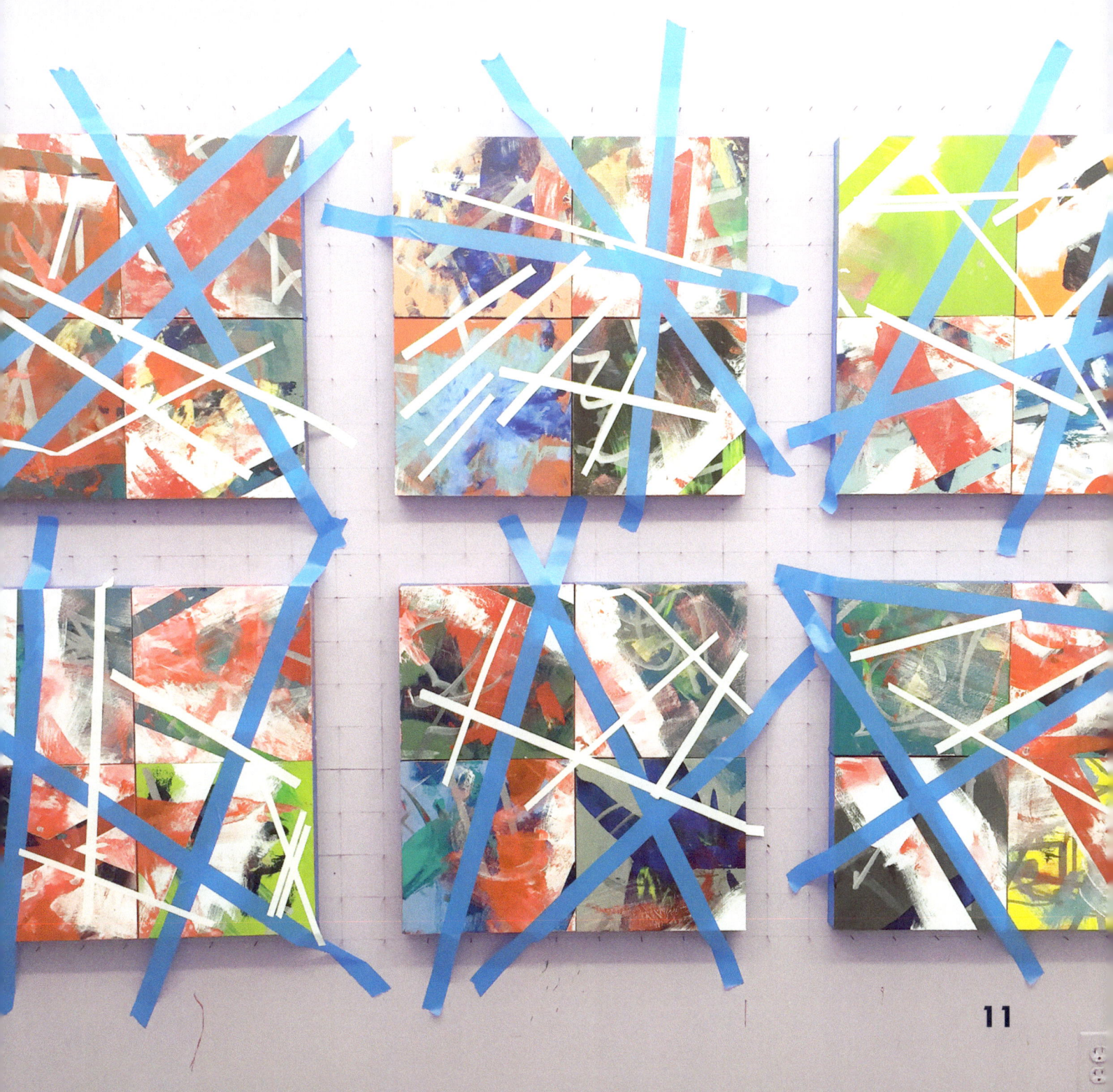

11

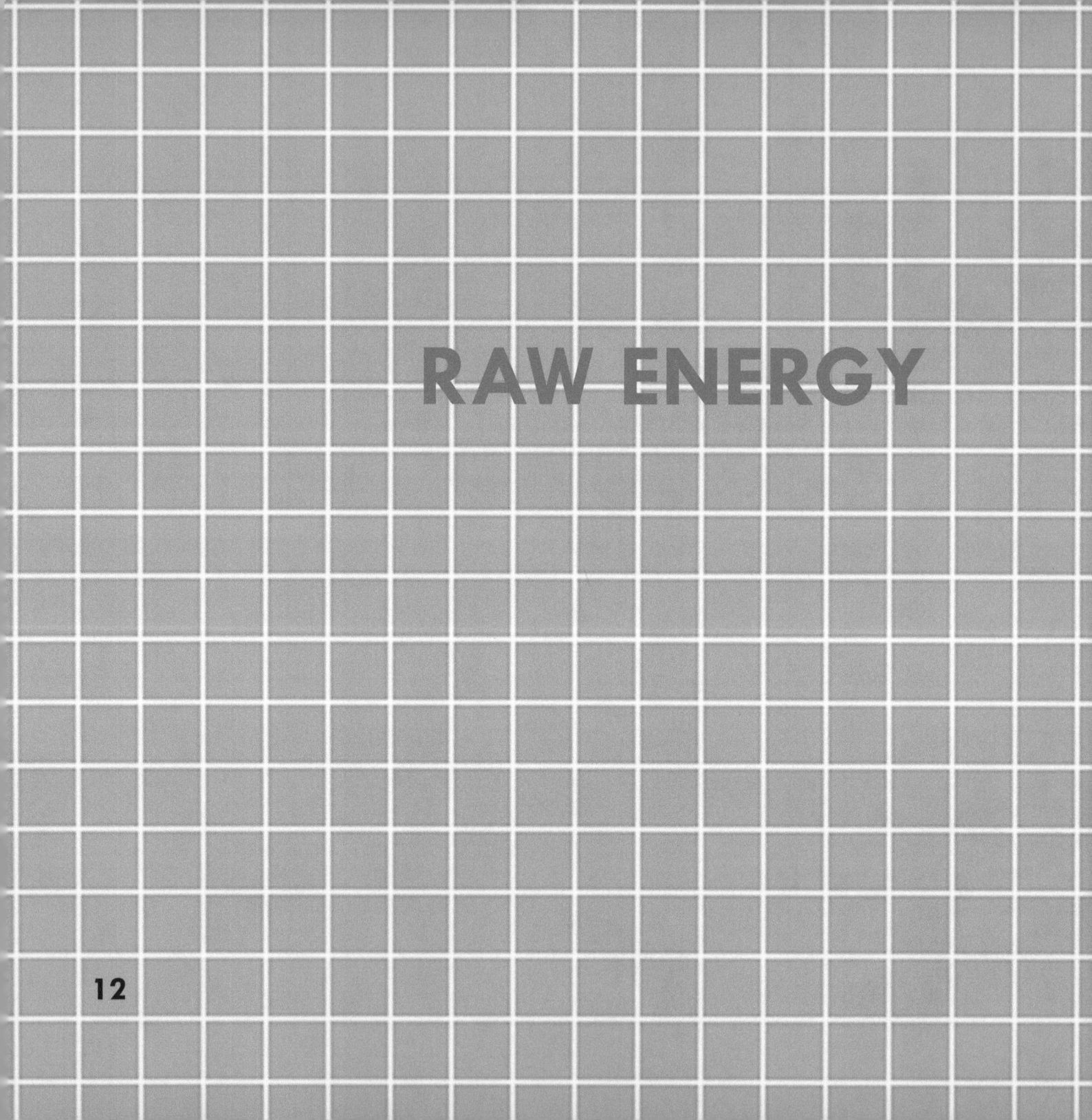

RAW ENERGY

12

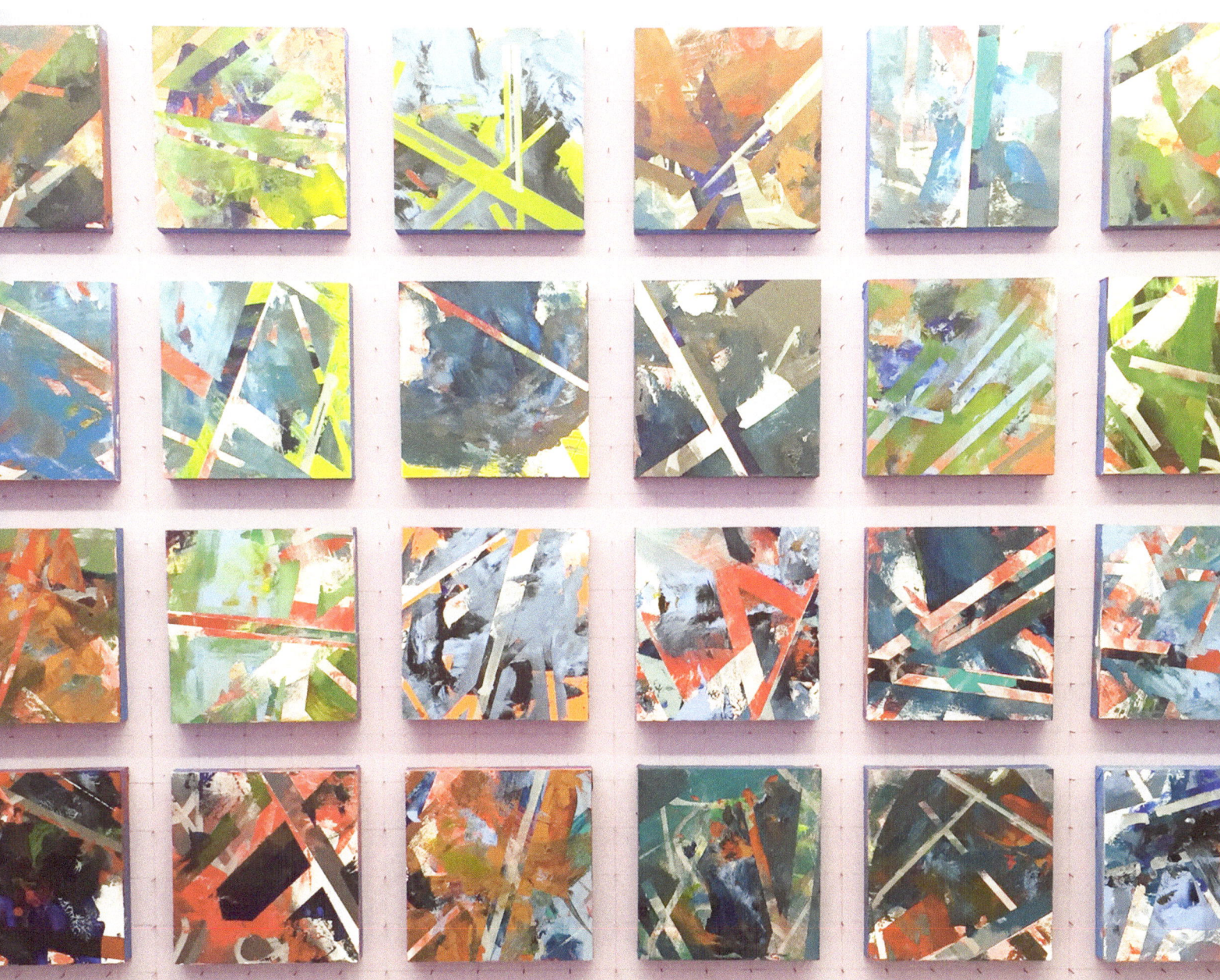

13

EXPERIMENTAL STACKS

14

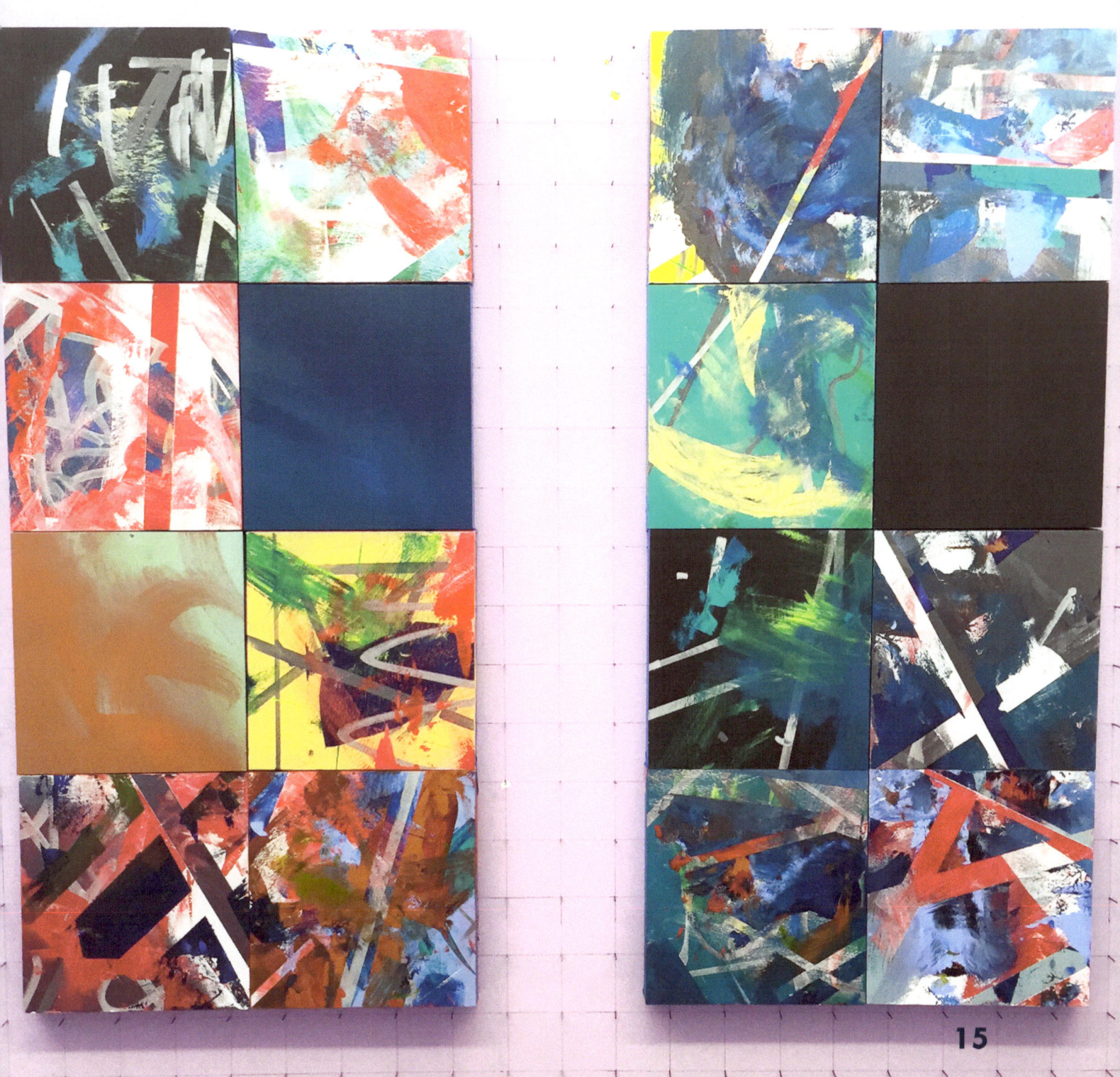

VISCERAL
JAMBALAYA

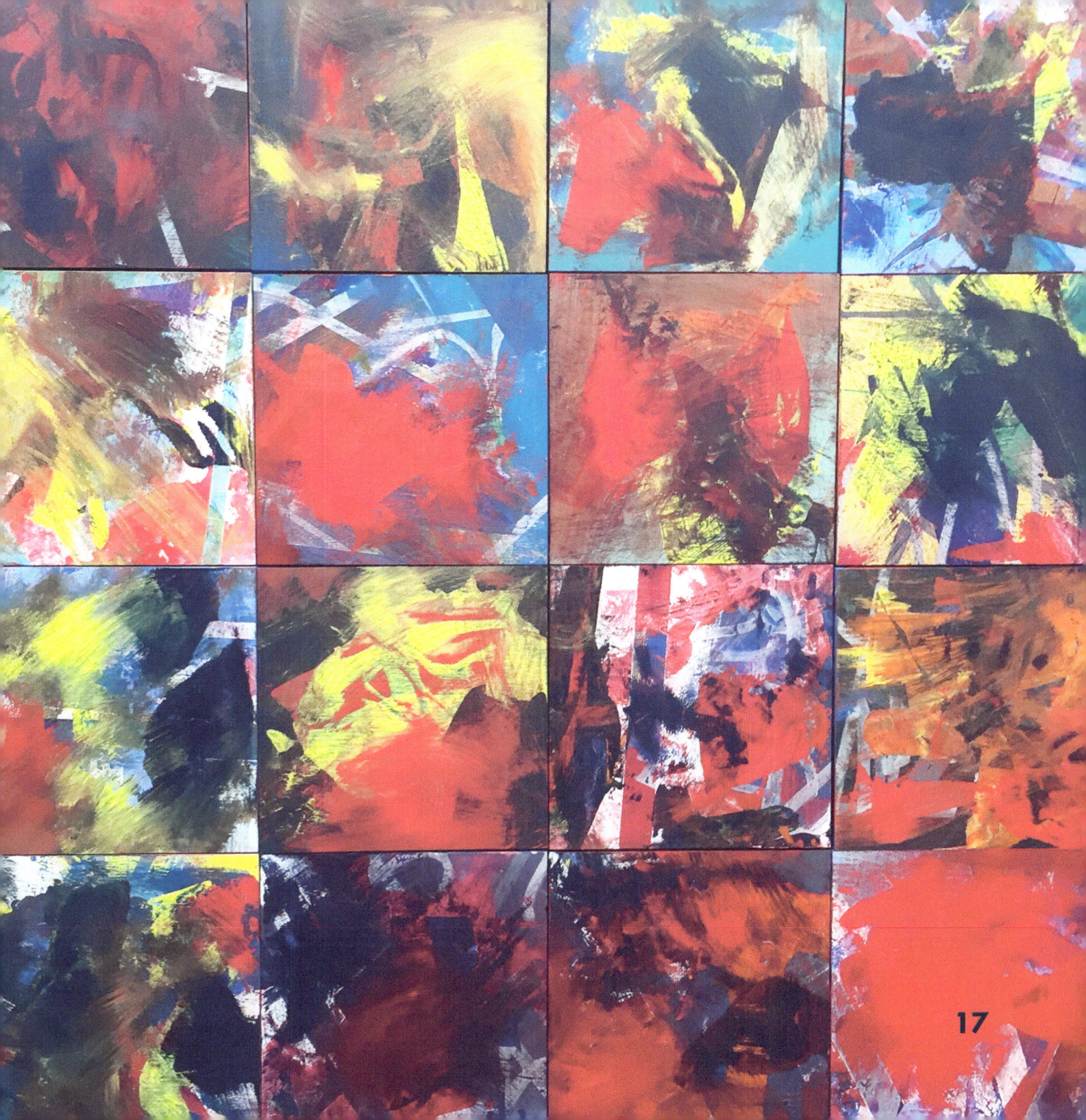

17

YEAR OF
THE
ROOSTER

18

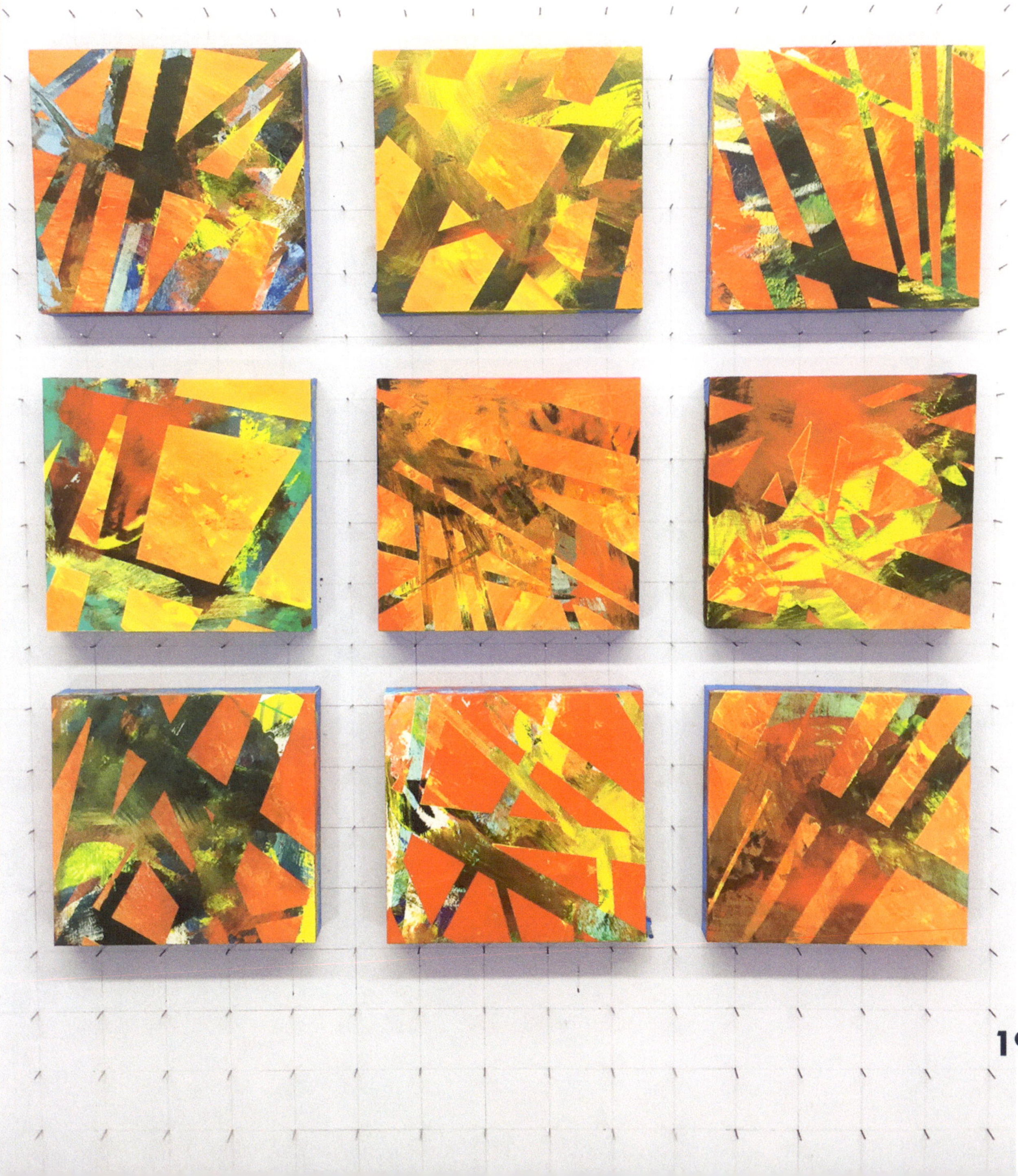

ATTACK MODE

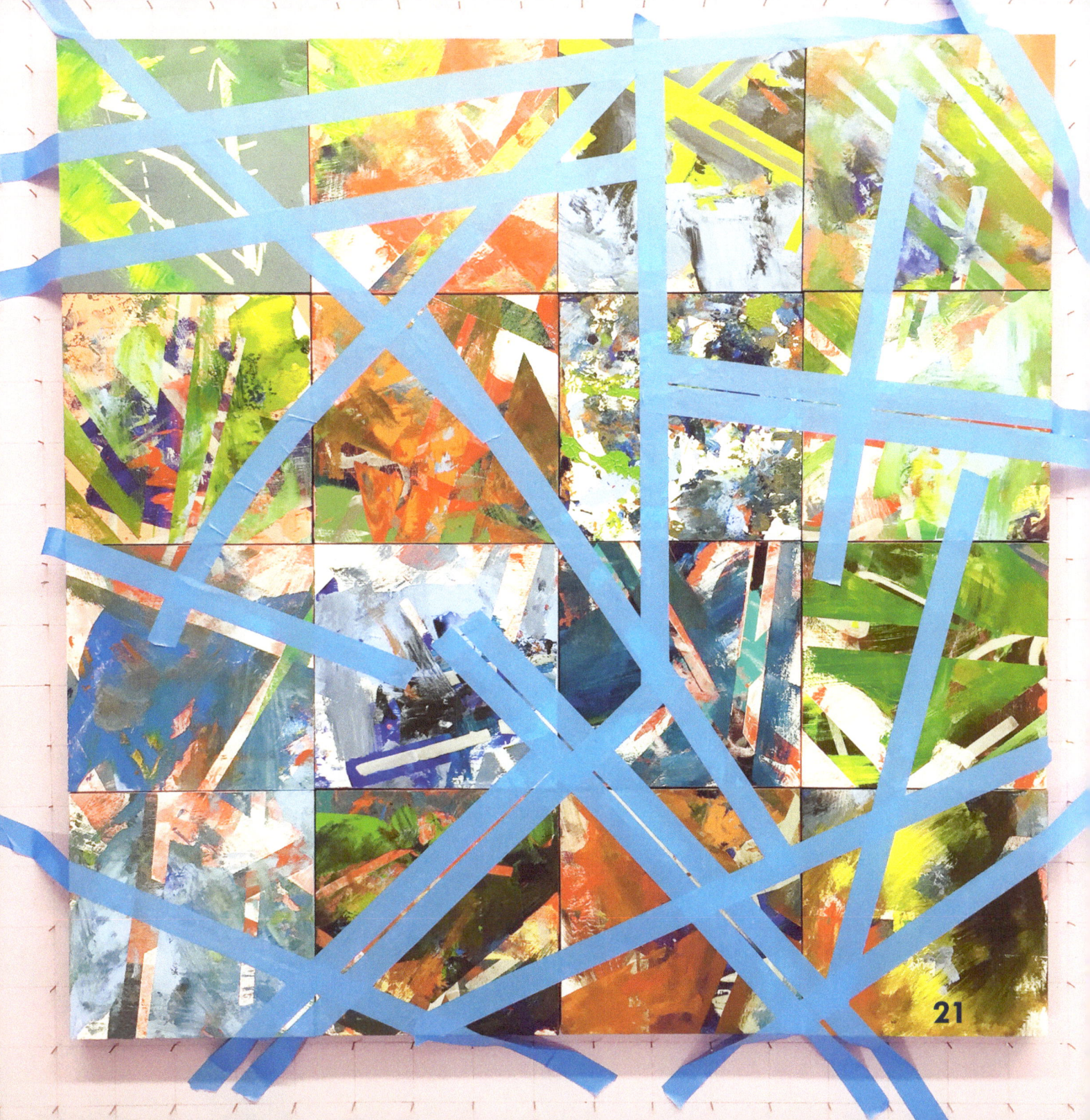

21

CINEMATIC STORYBOARDS

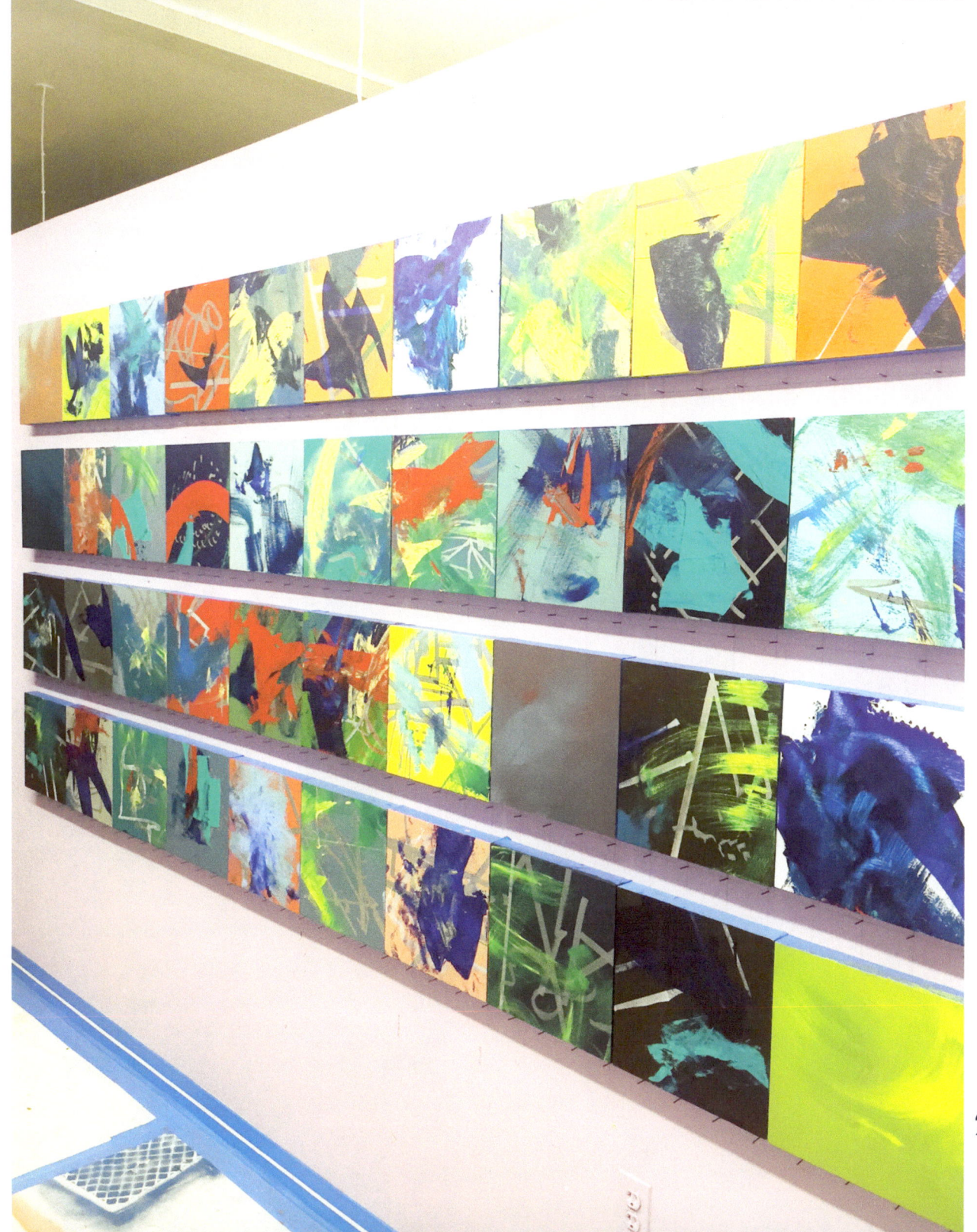

23

DECONSTRUCTING
CONSTRUCTIVISM

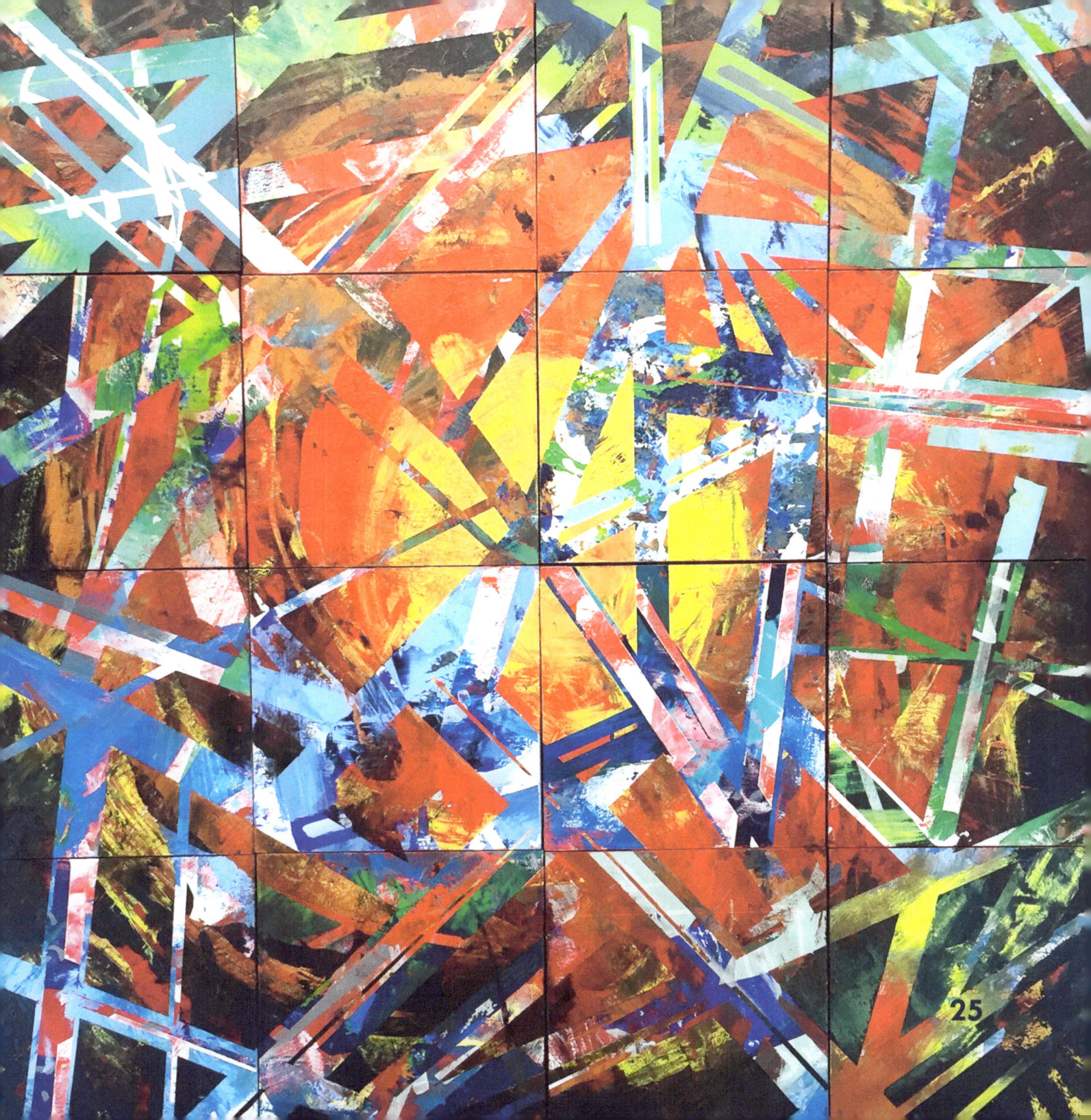

25

URBAN RAMIFICATIONS, RECYCLED SIDE PROJECT

26

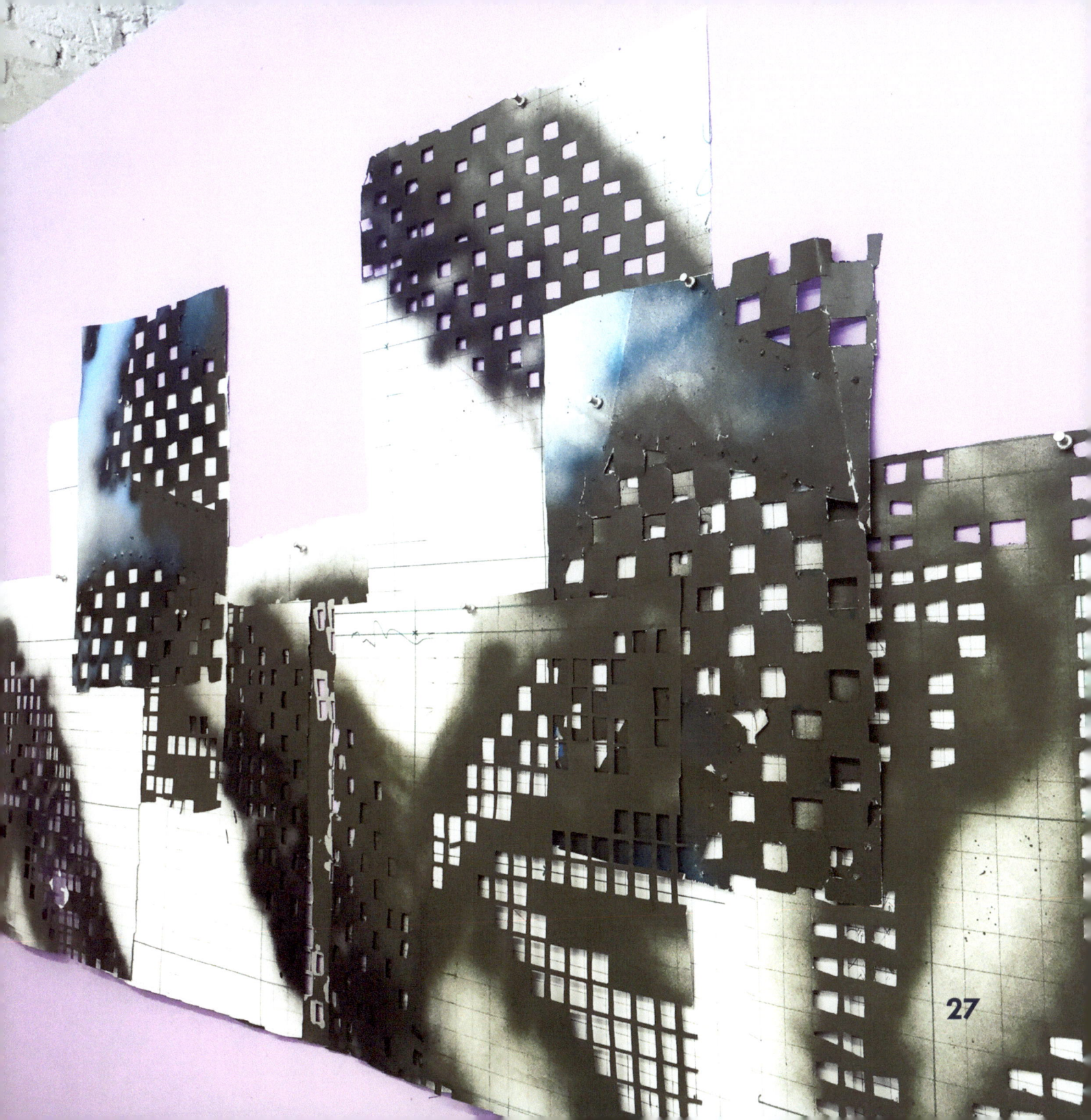

27

COMBINED SERIES, ADVANCING PIECES AND A COUPLE OF FRONT RUNNERS

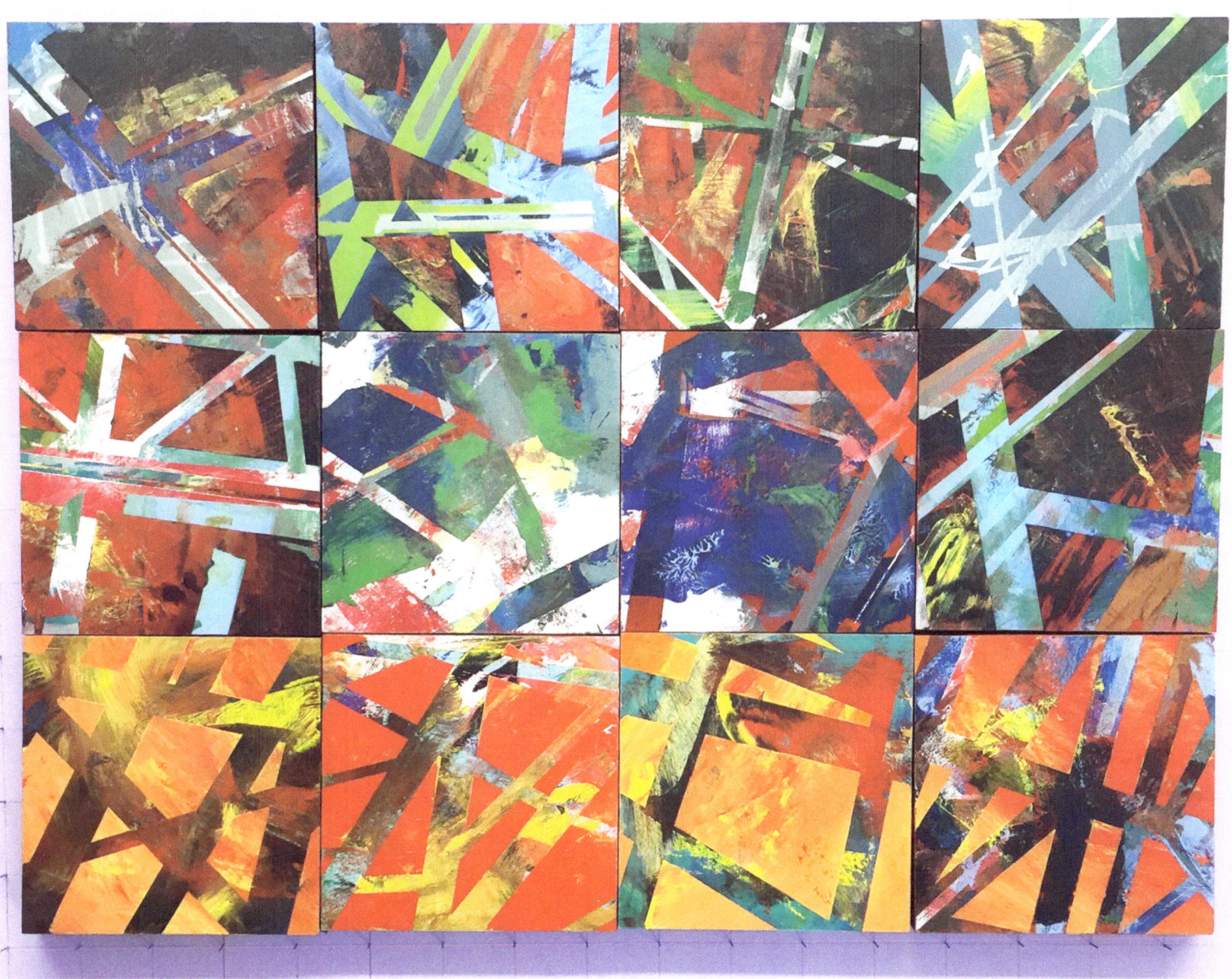

AND A LOT MORE
JUST TO SEE
WHAT IT LOOKS LIKE

30

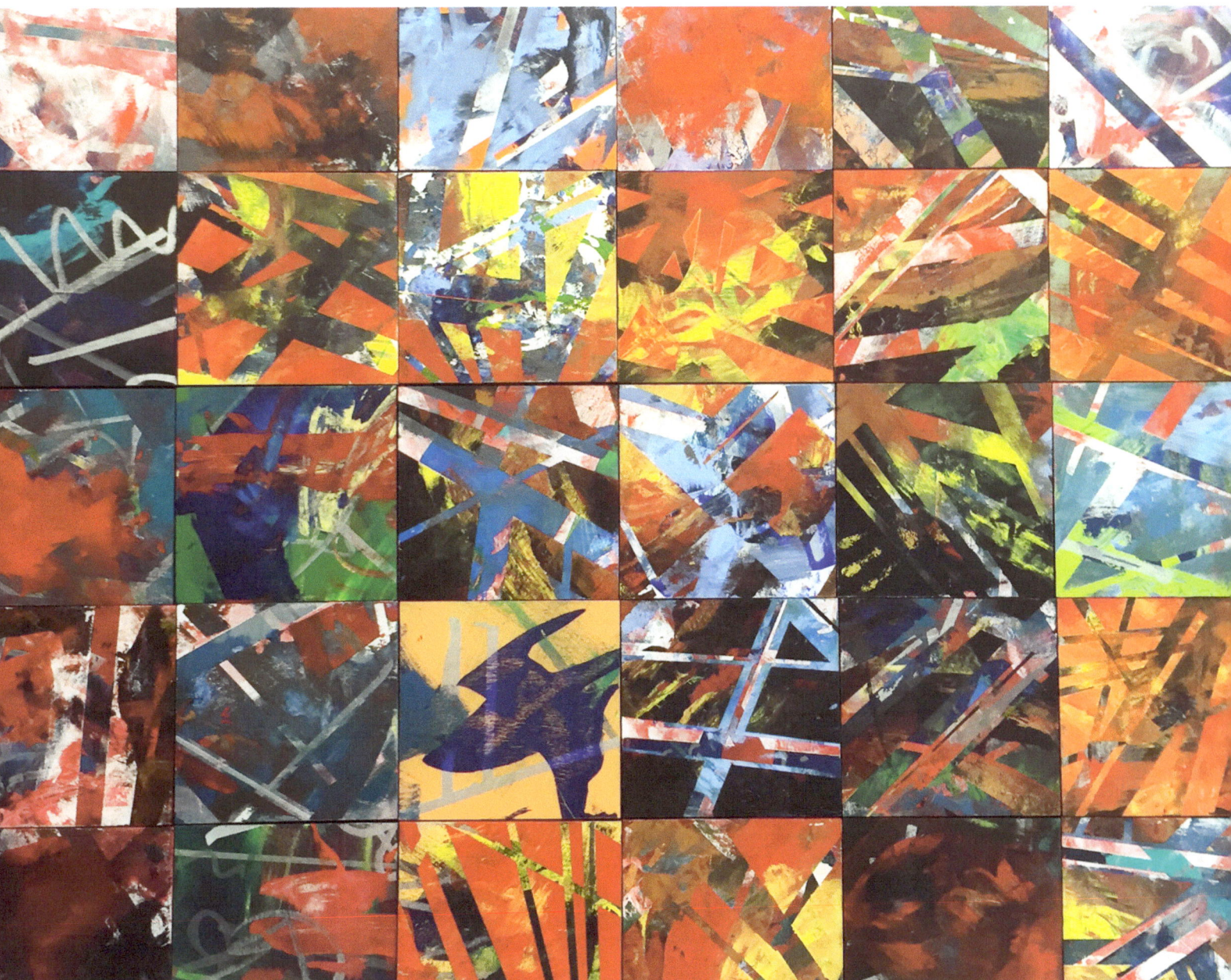

PORTRAYING VECTOR SPACE

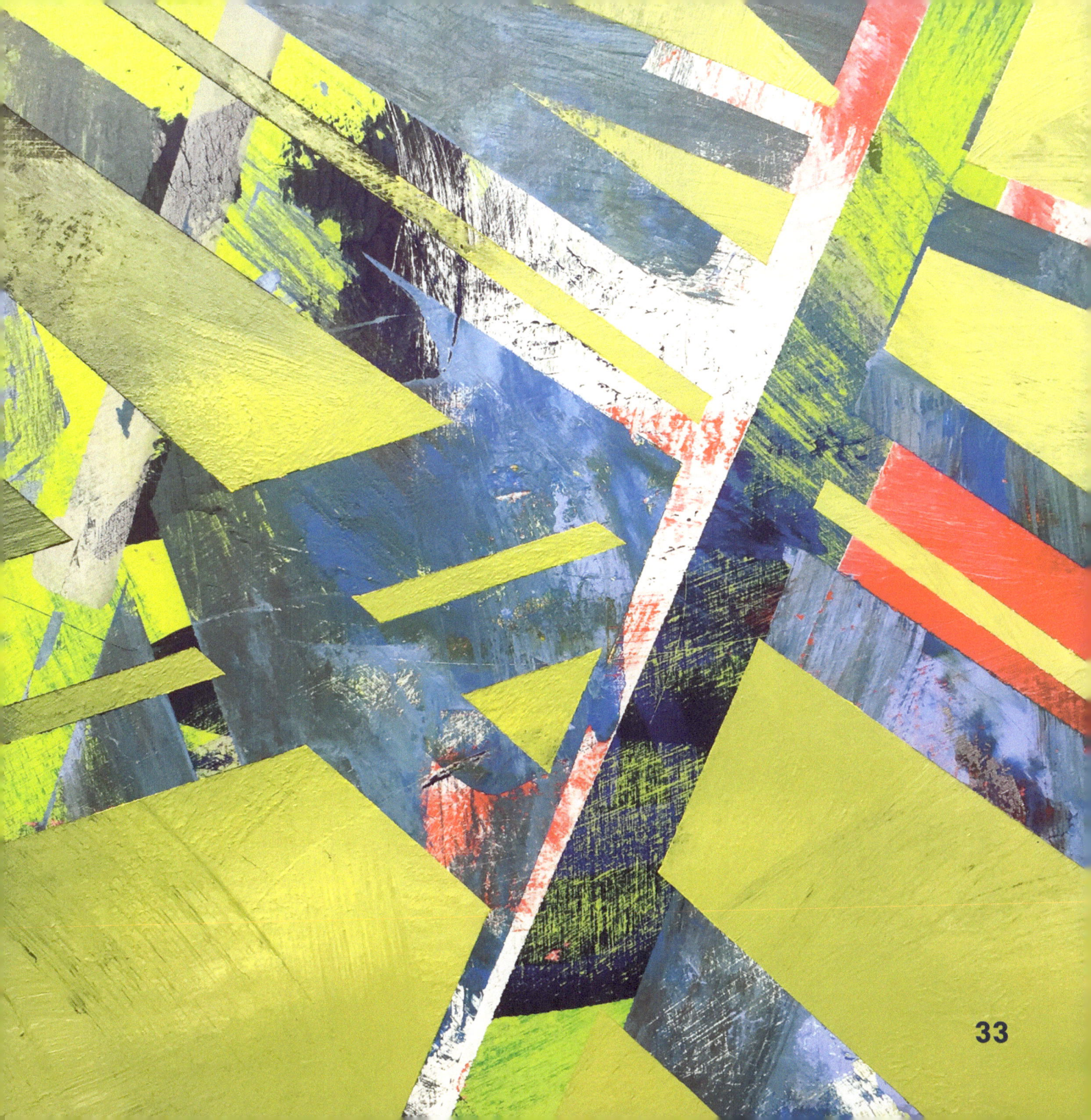

33

ITERATIONS

34

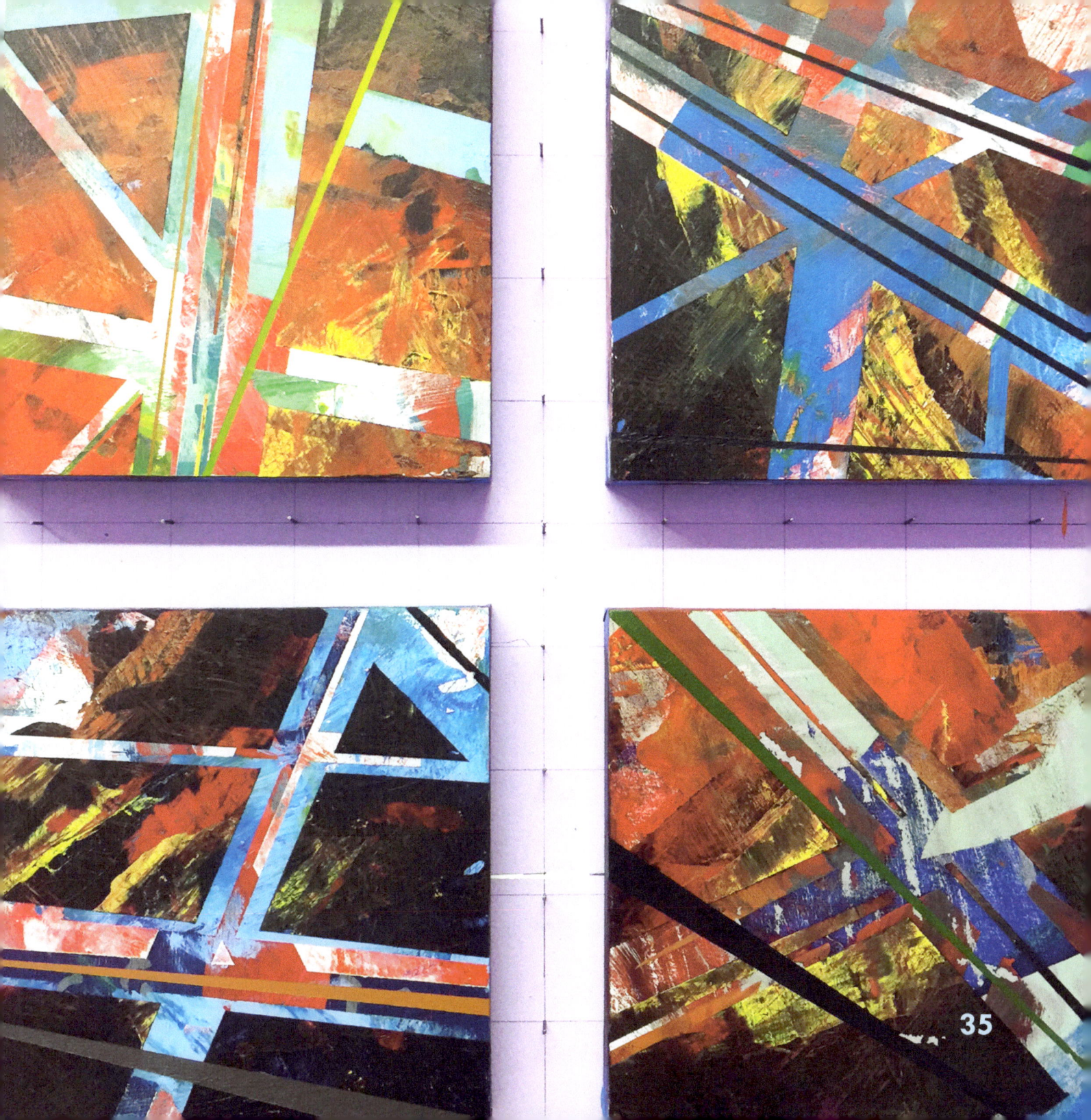

LOVE AND RISK

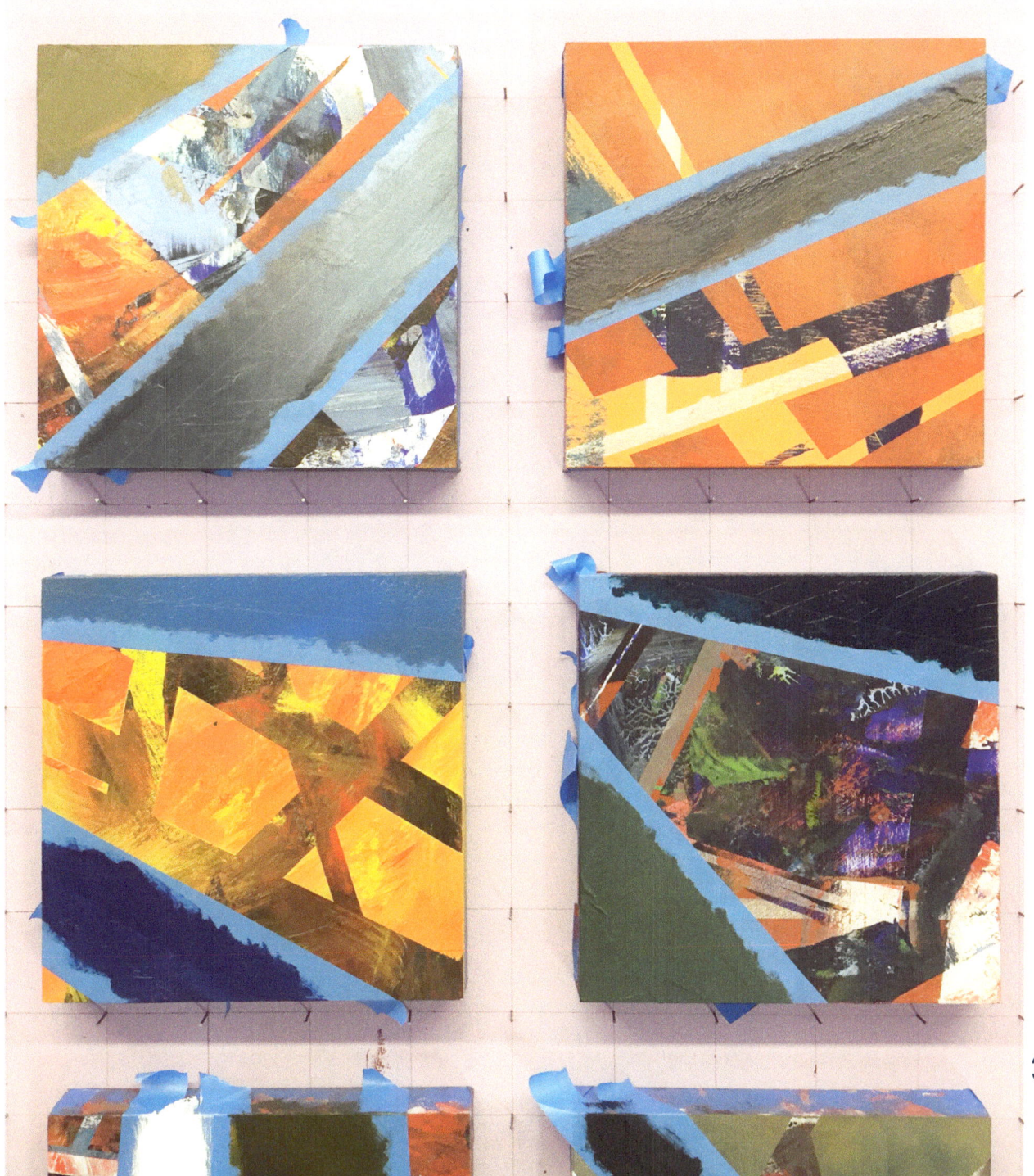

PLAYFUL
IMMERSION

38

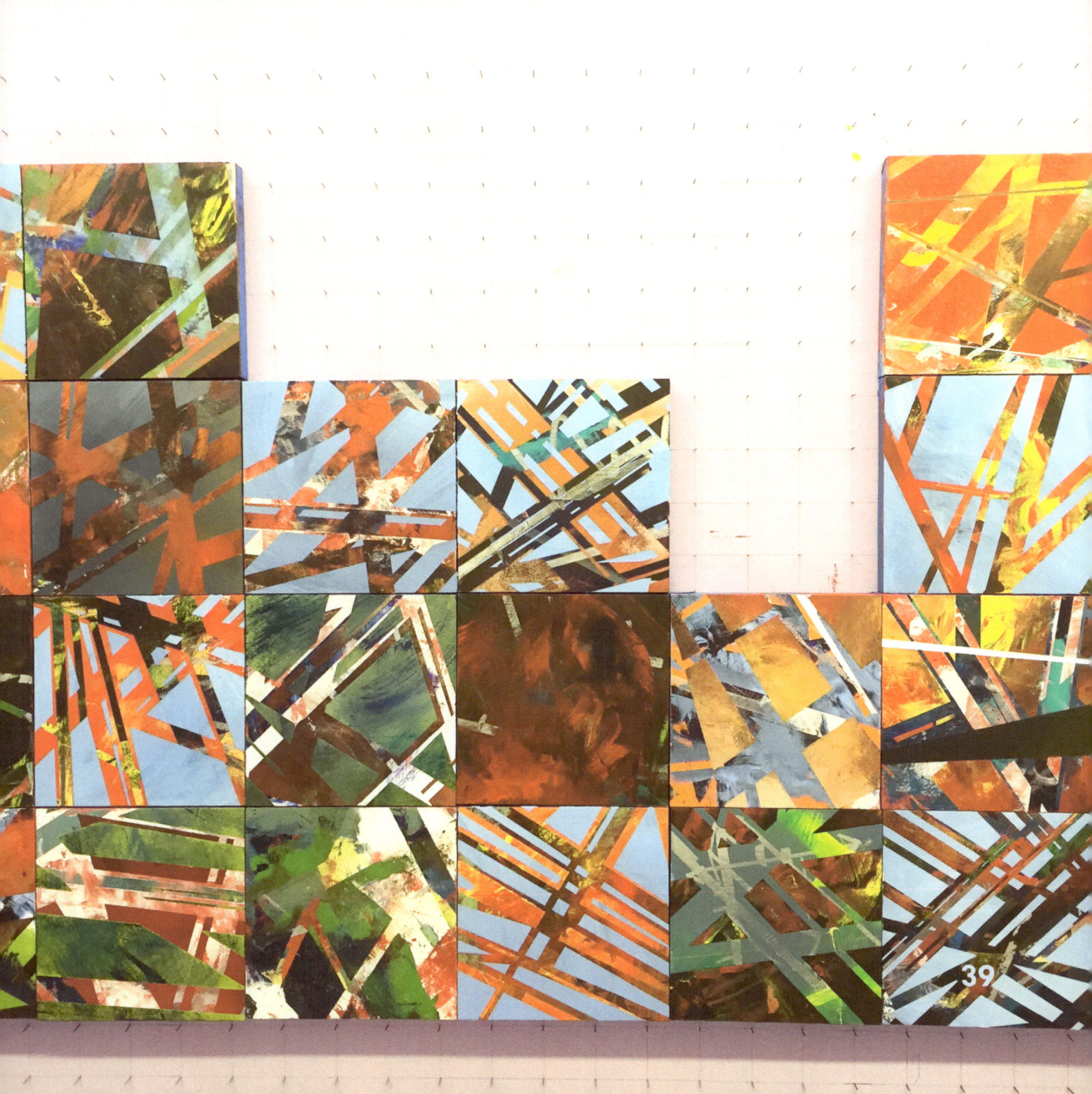

39

VECTOR NORMALIZATION

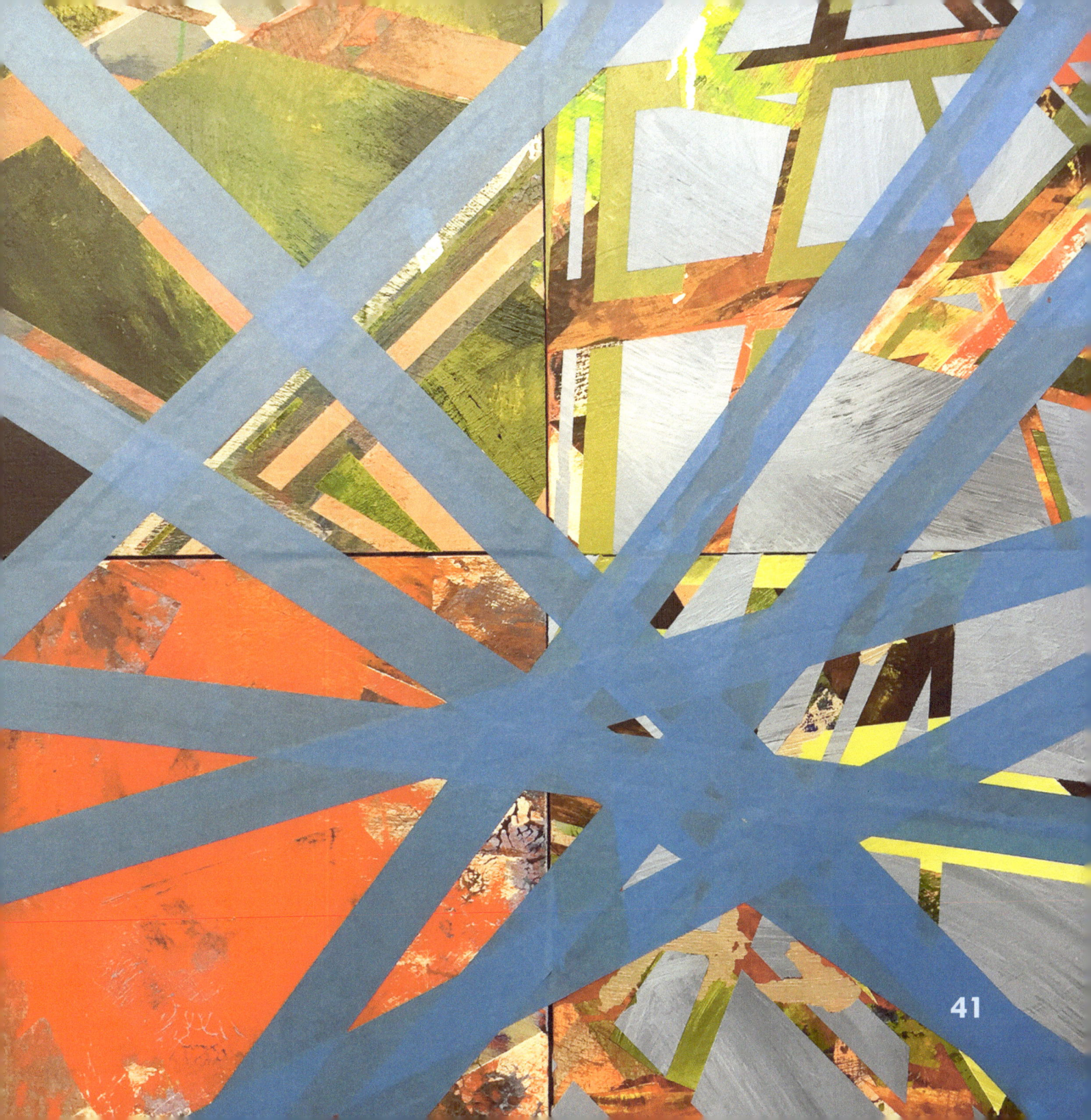

41

ETHEREAL

42

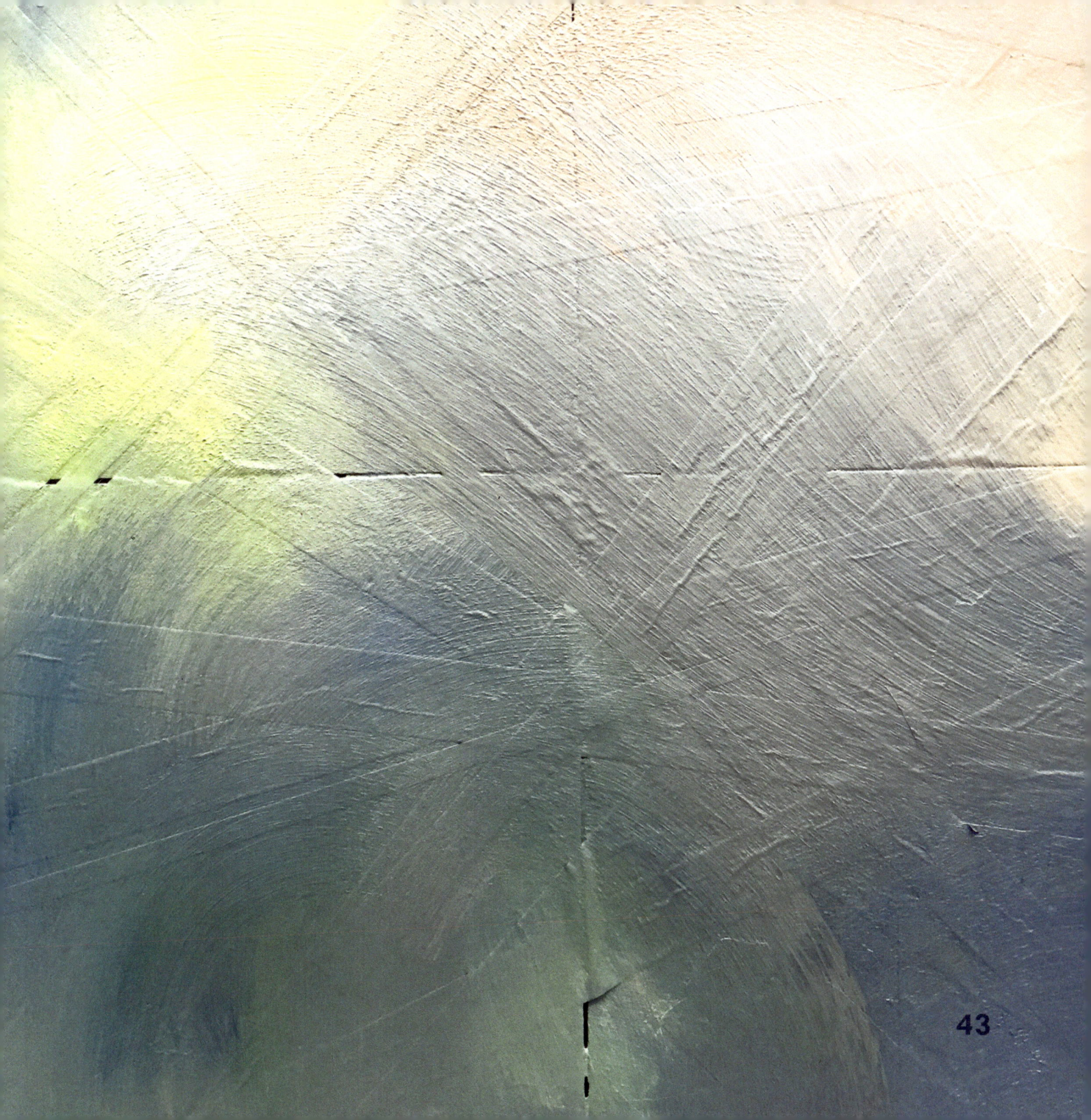

43

PAINTERLY
PHILOSOPHY

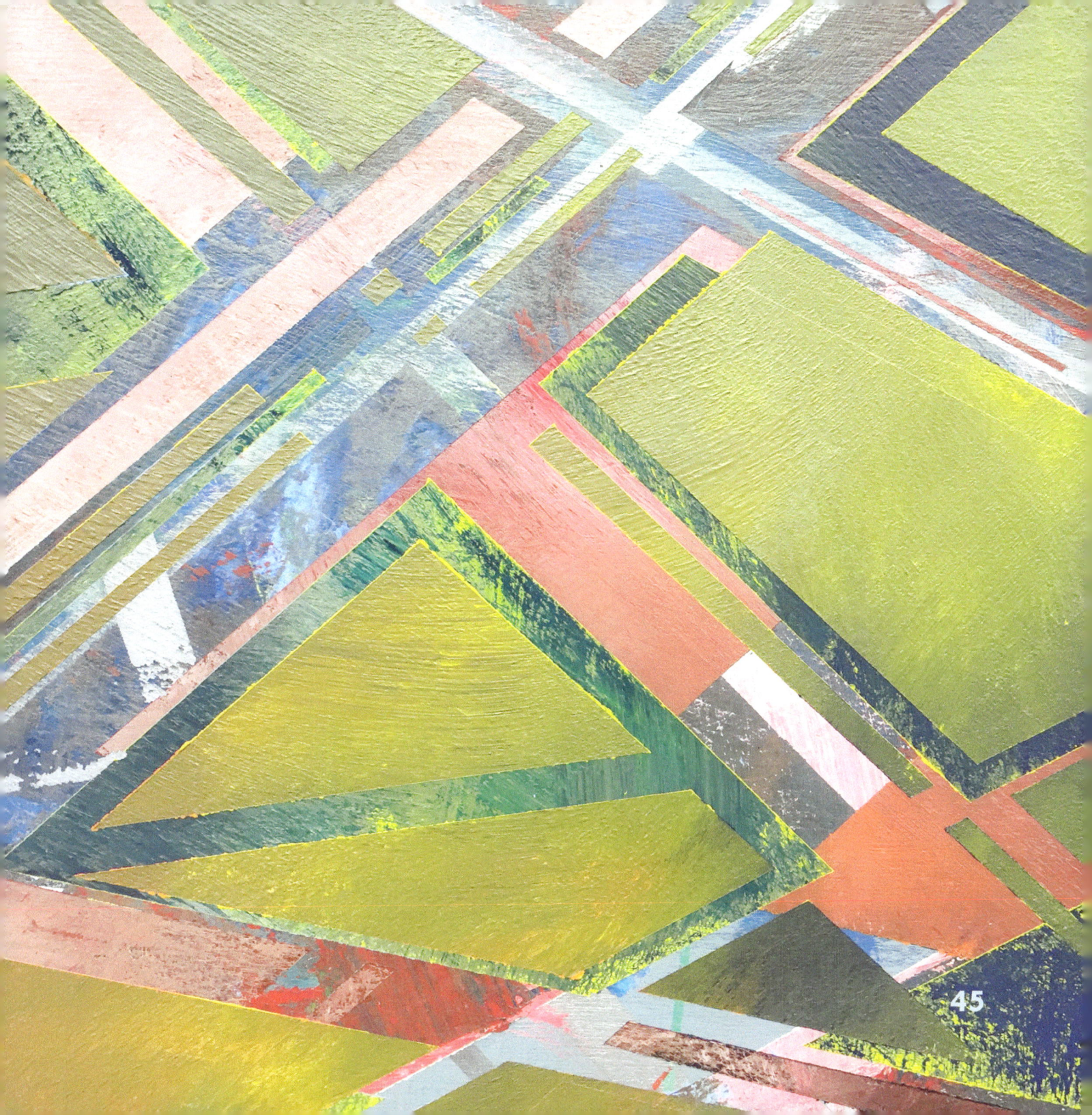
45

MAGMATRONIC
PROTOTYPE

46

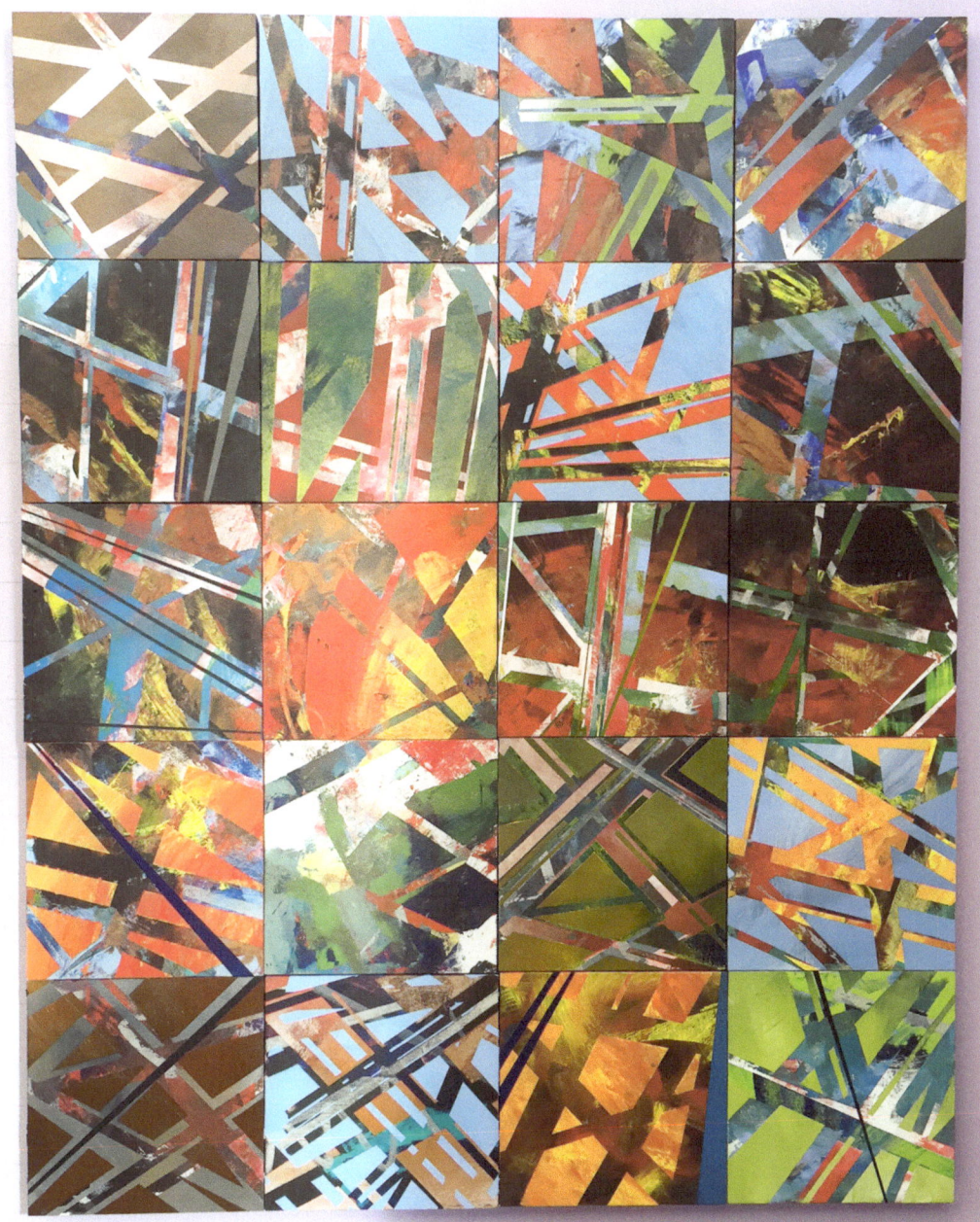

MORE

48

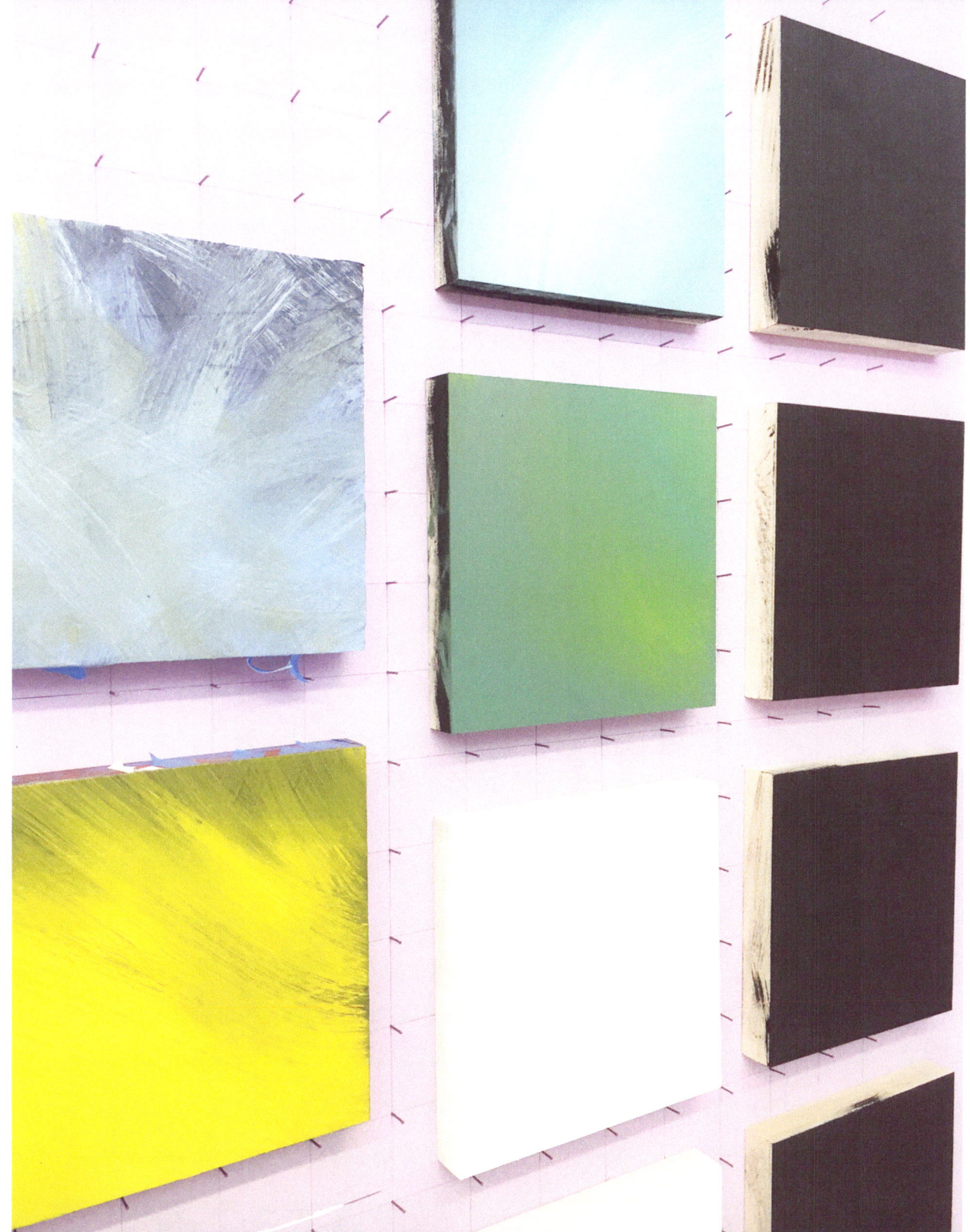

49

EXPANDING LAYERS, RAISING THE BAR

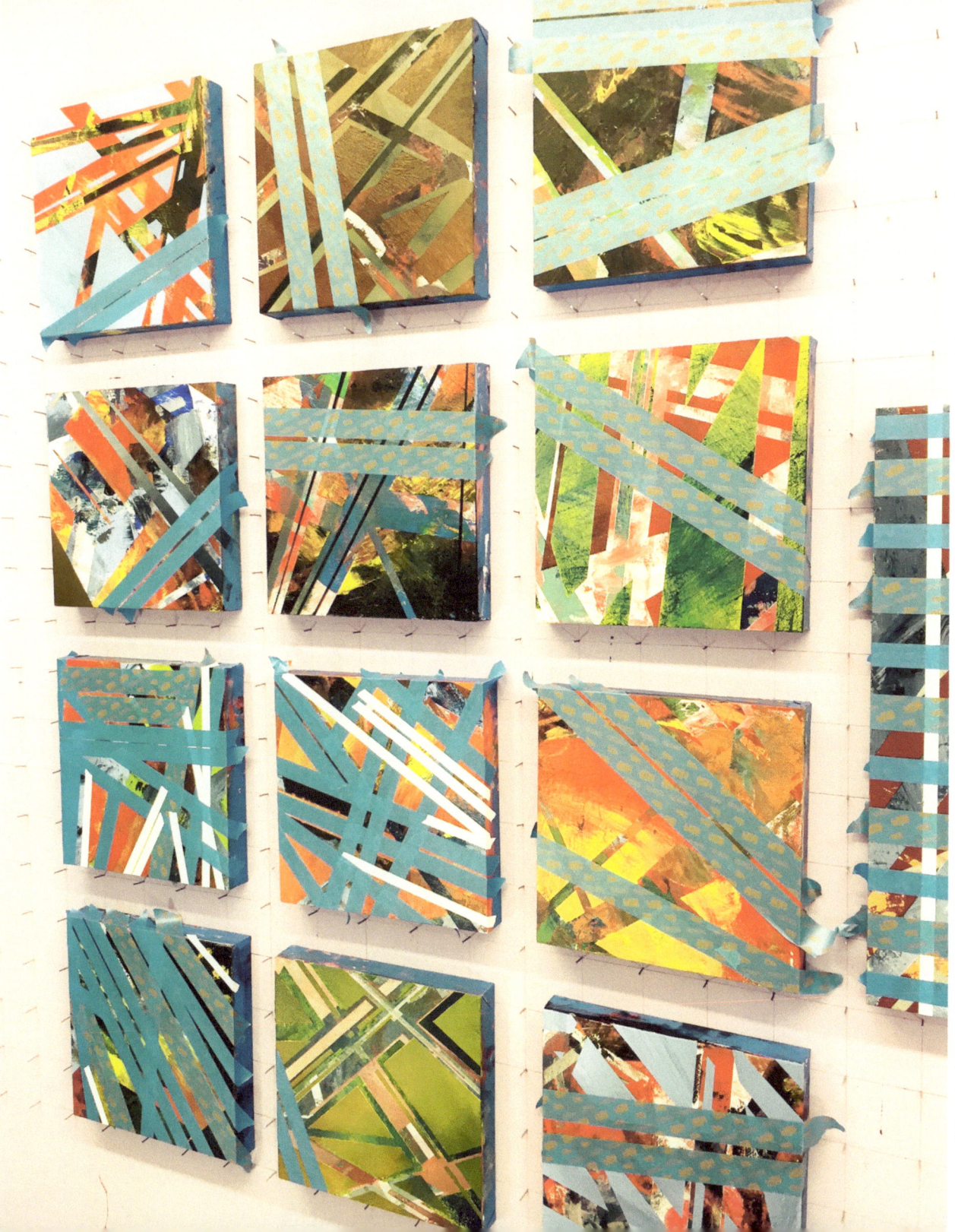

CRUCIBLE OF CONTINUITY

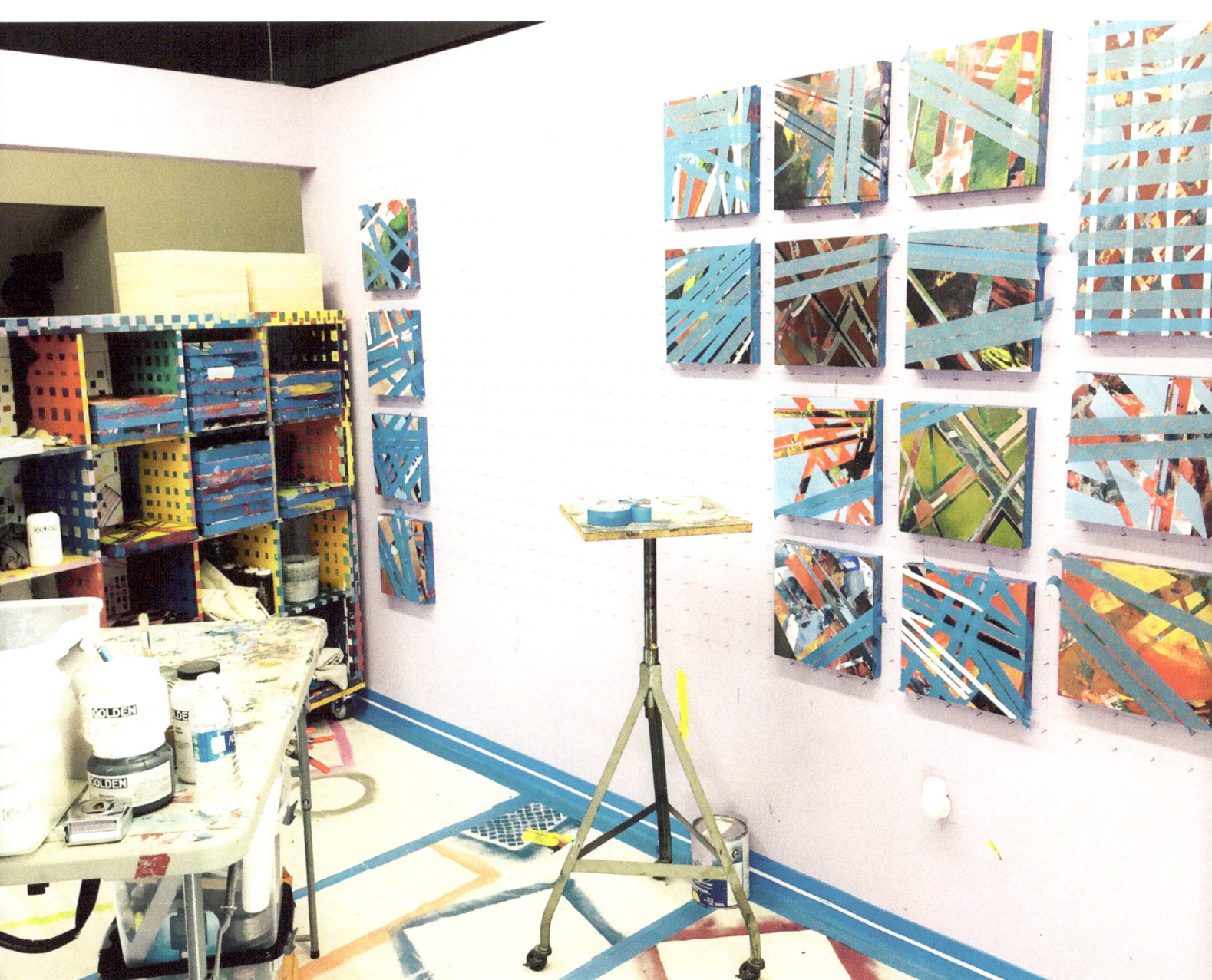

ROGUES' GALLERY

54

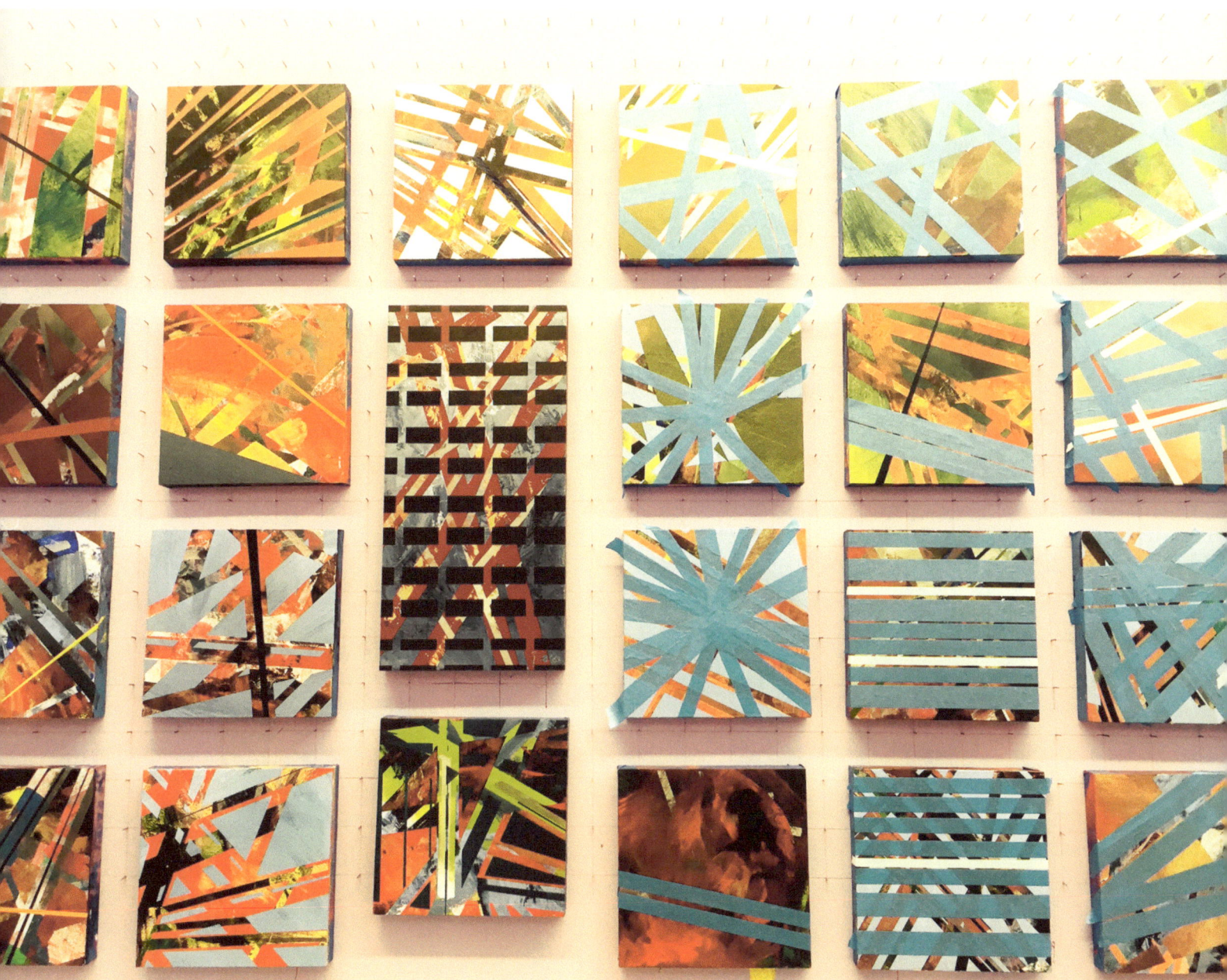

INTERSUBJECTIVE TRANSFERENCE

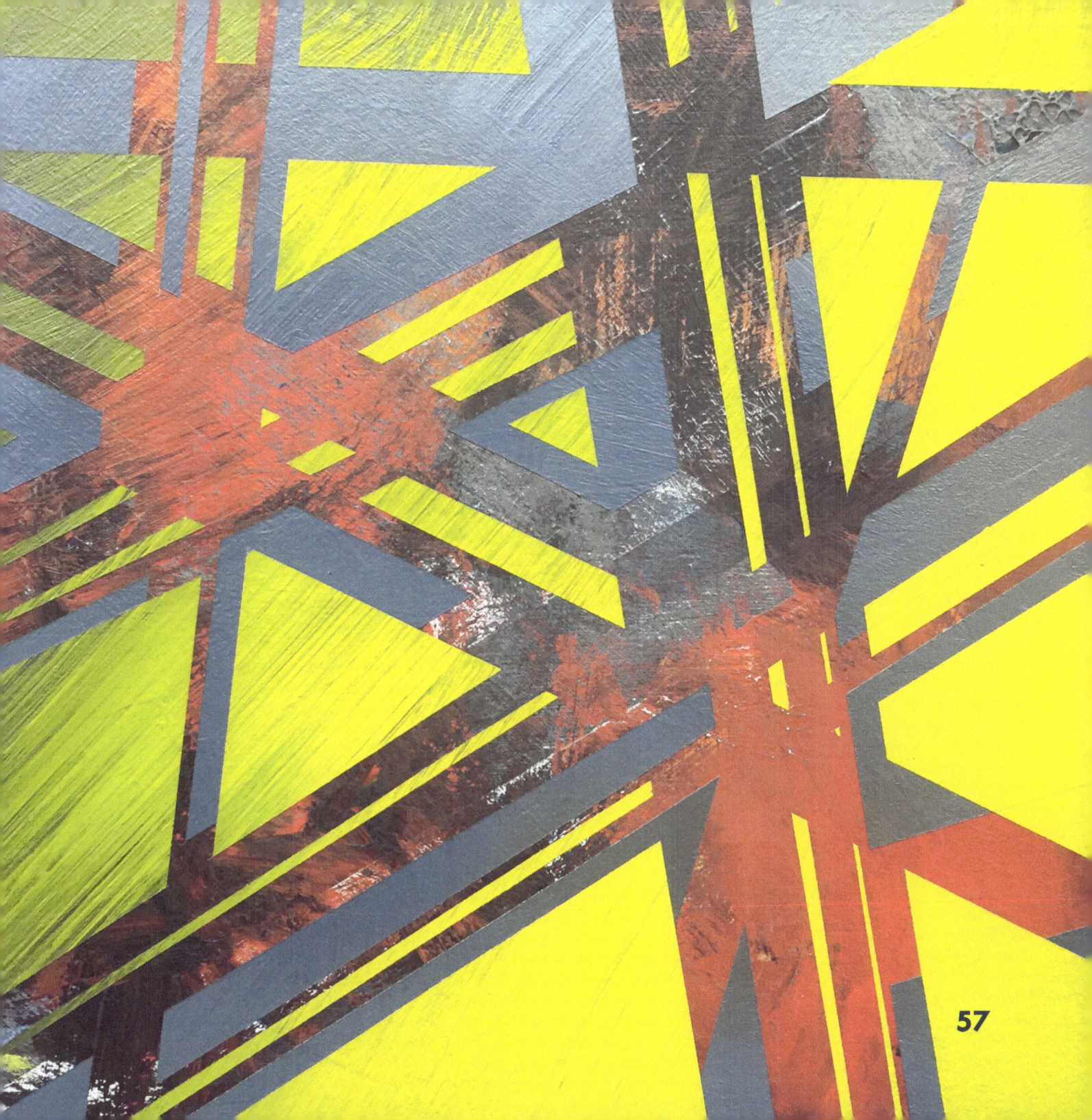

57

RELATIONAL
DATABASE

58

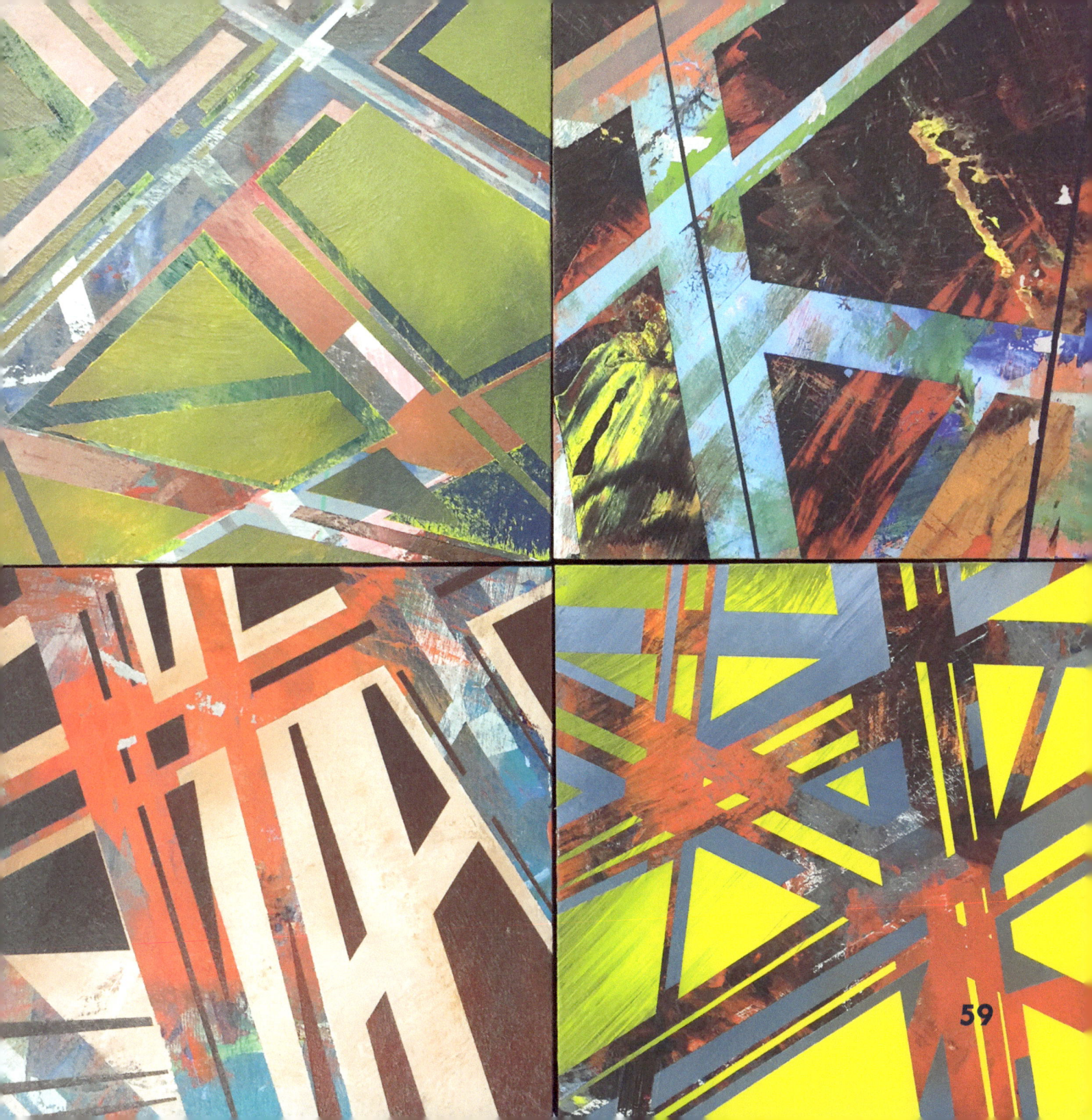

59

BUILT
ENVIRONMENT

60

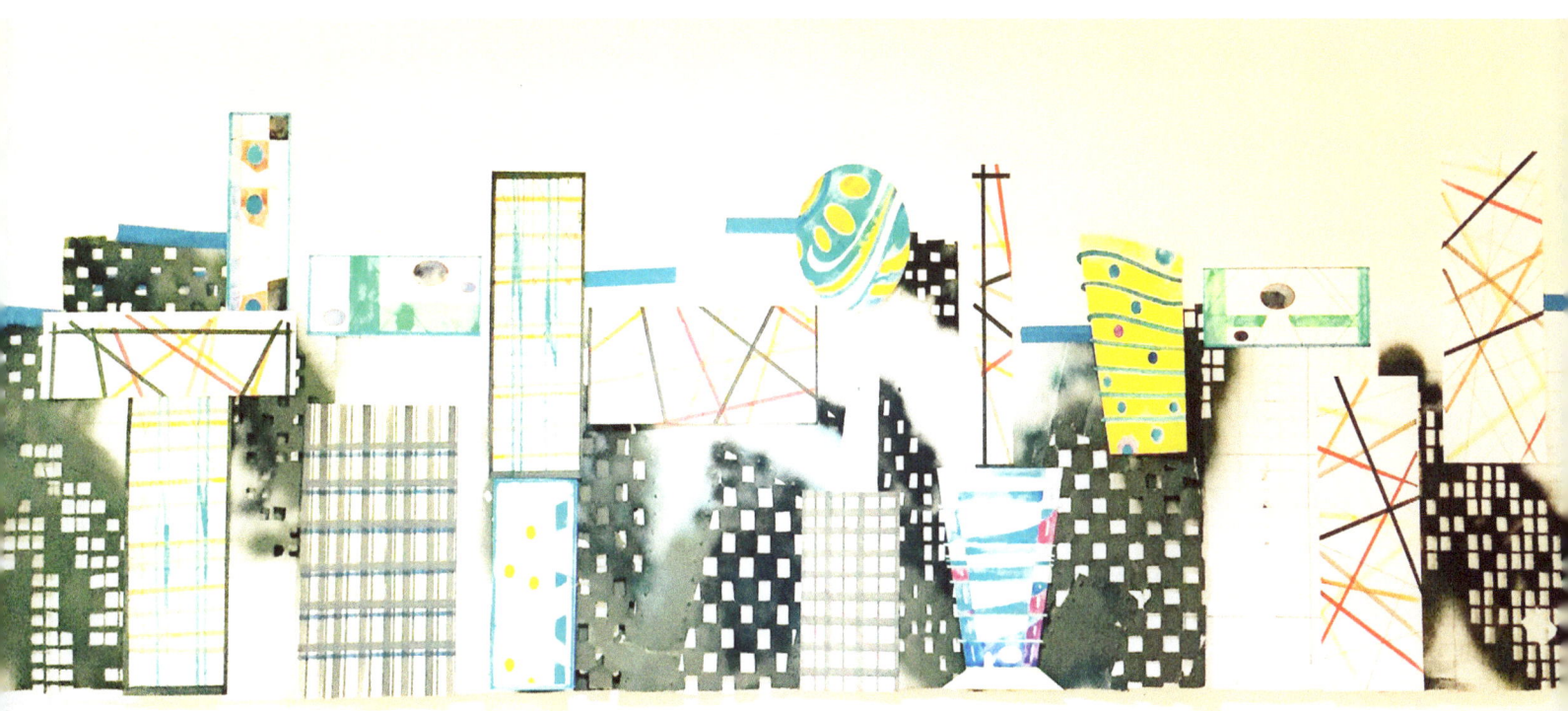

61

STUDIO
EVERY DAY

PHOTOS BY
BRENNAN LEE
TEDXJHU

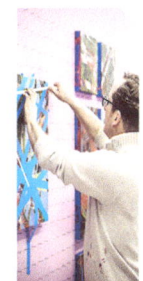
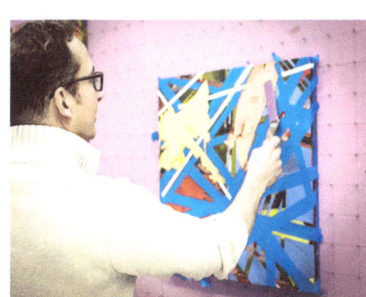
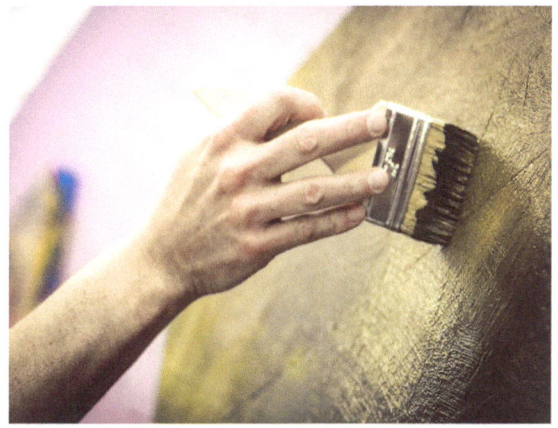
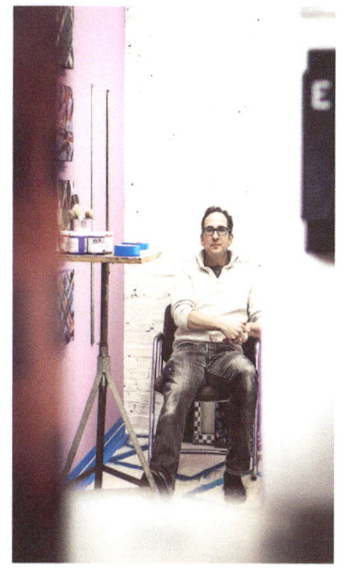
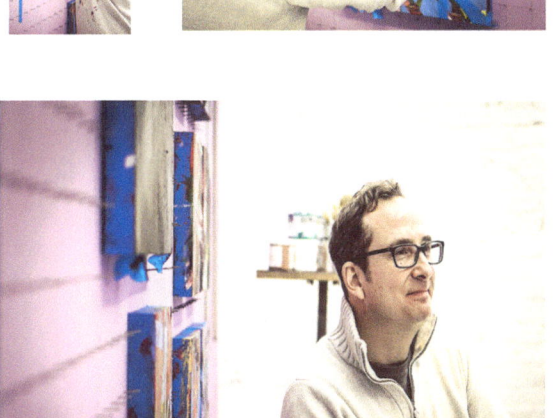
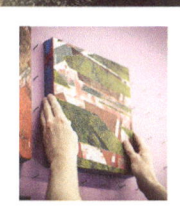
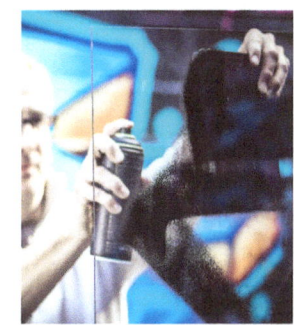
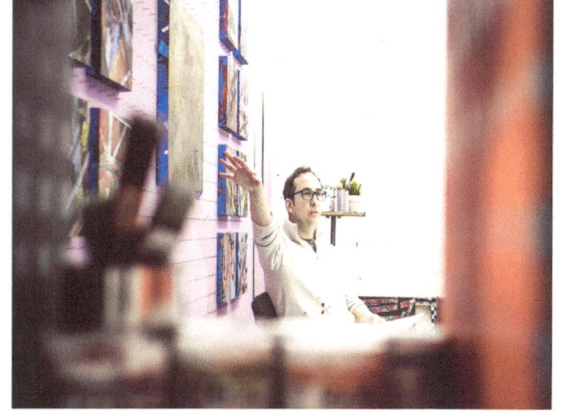
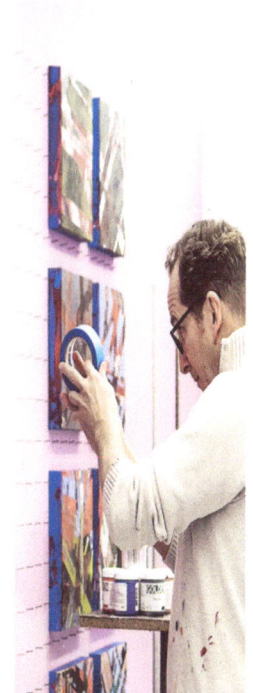
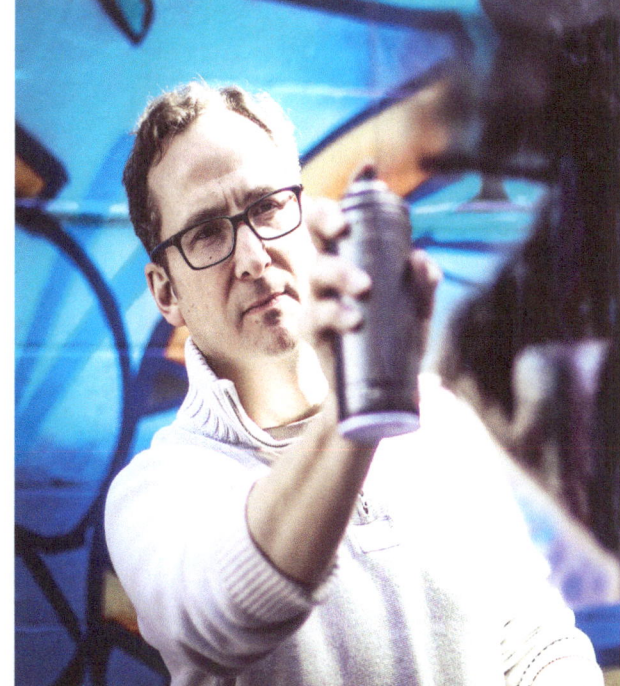
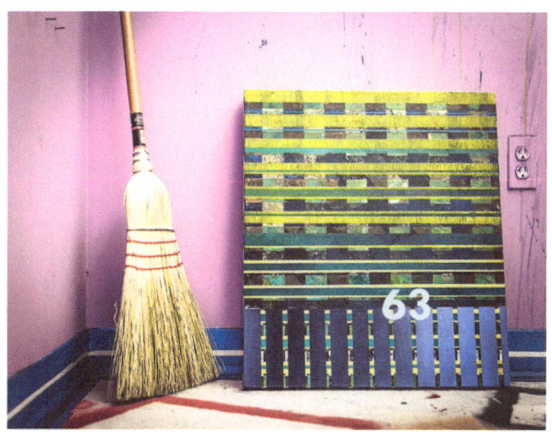

TEDXJHU

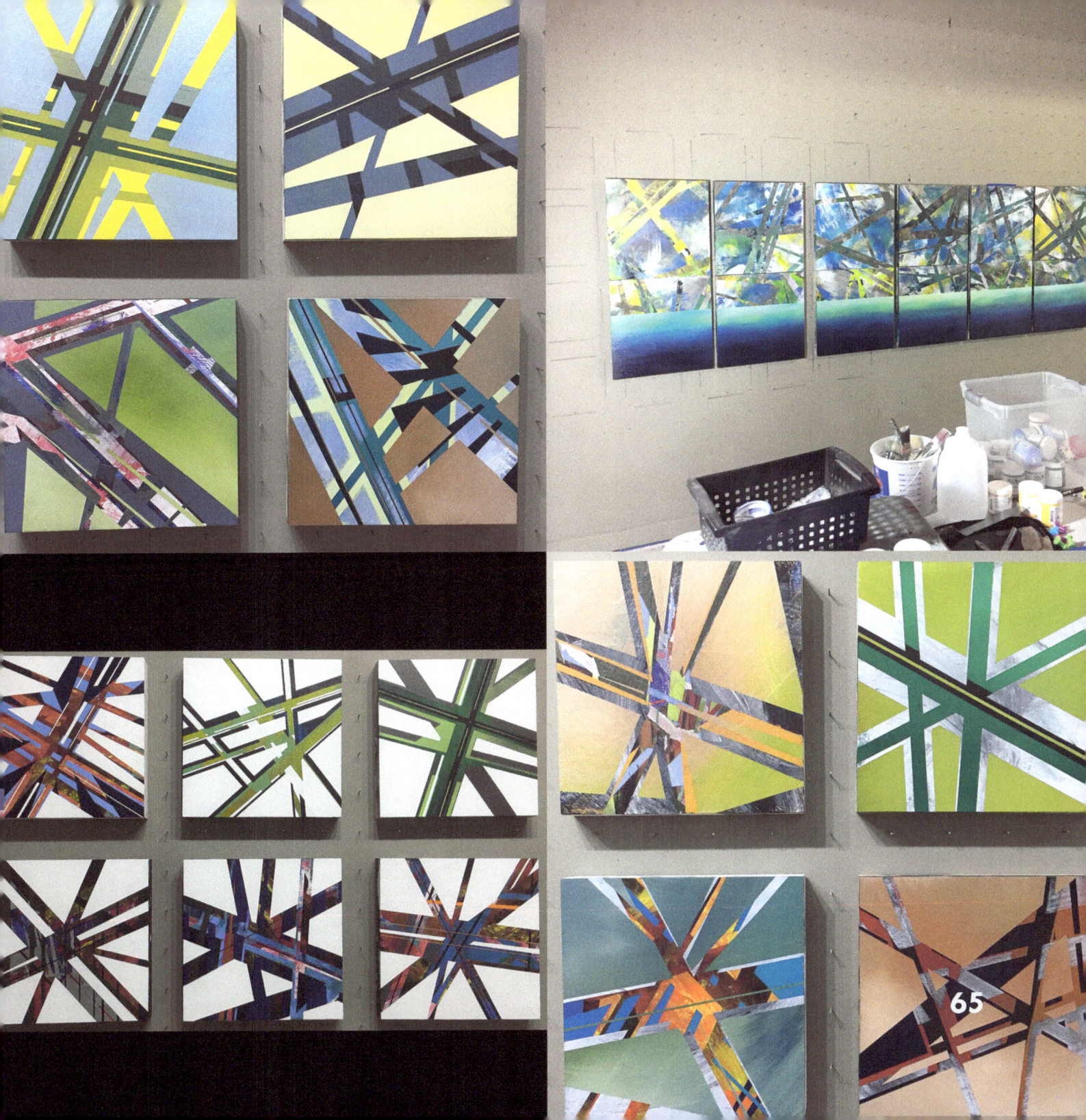

65

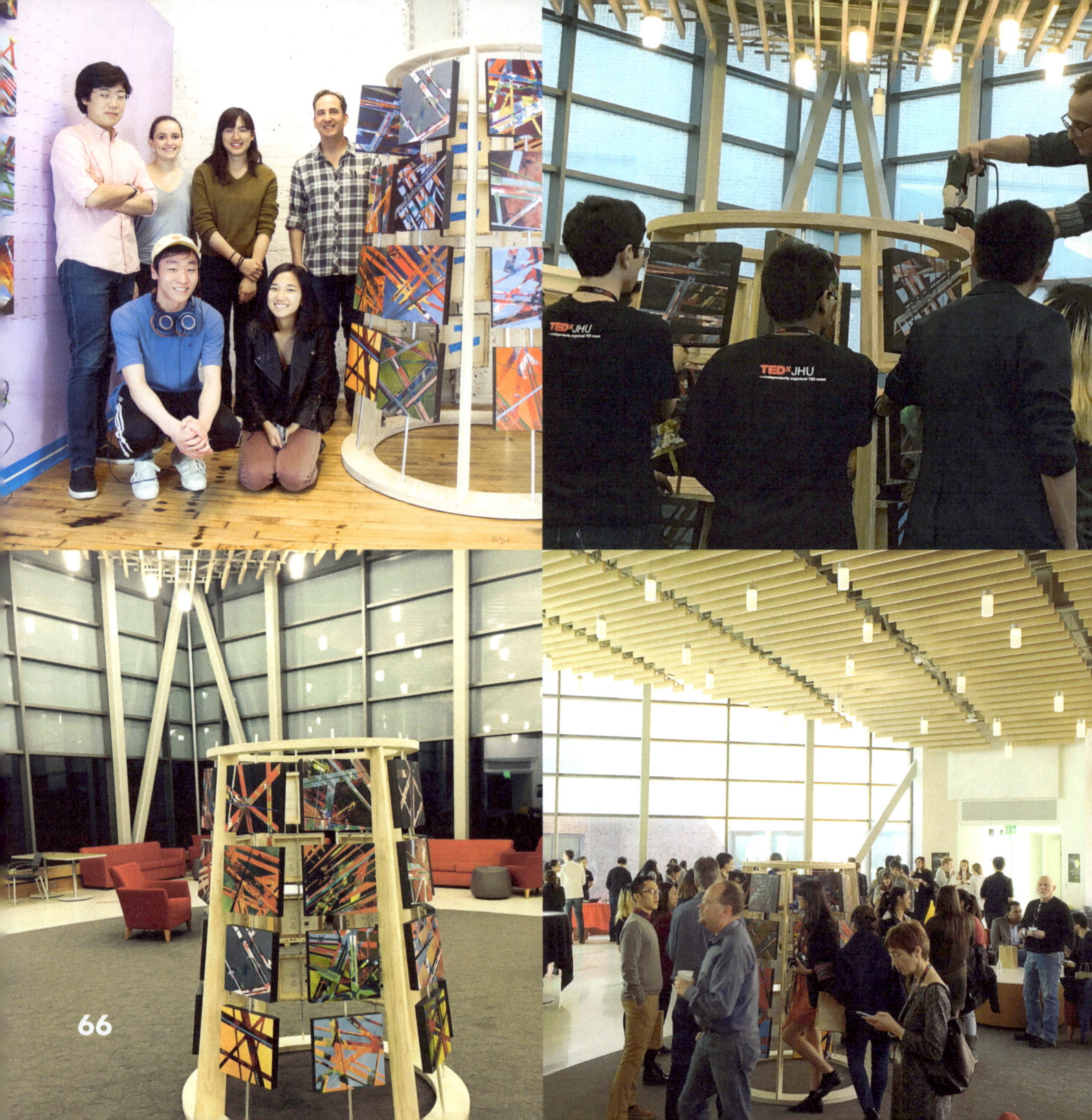

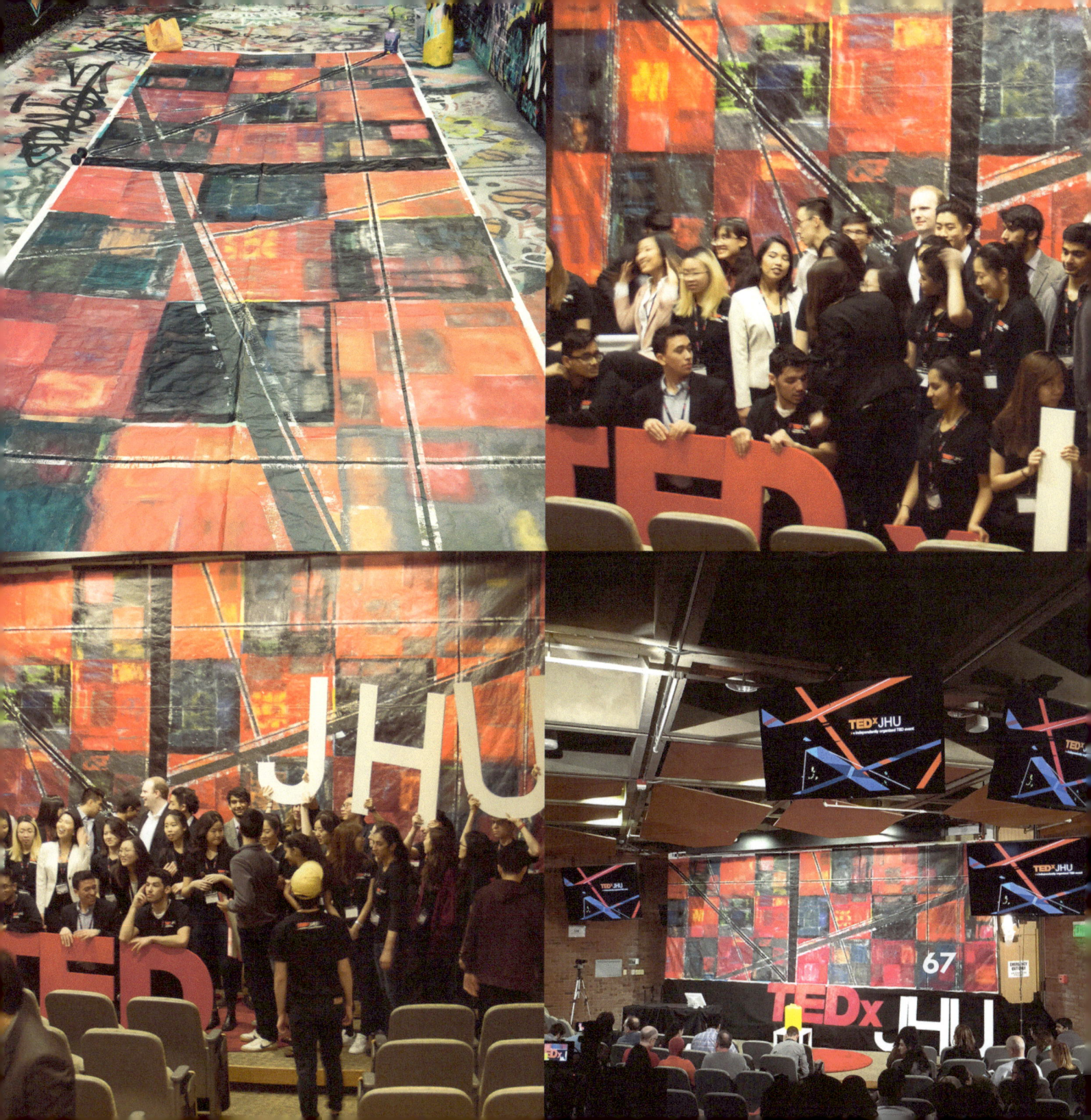

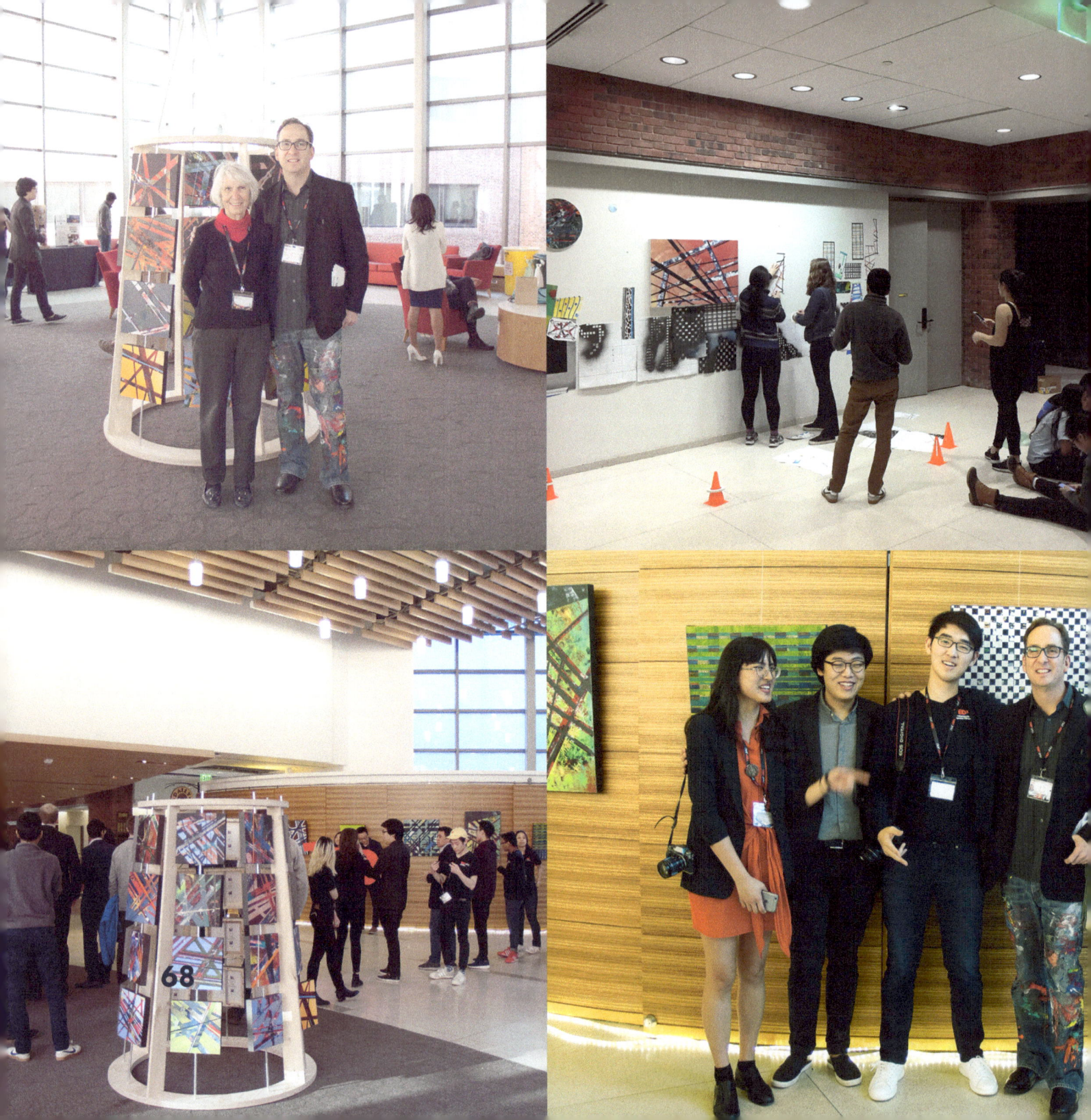

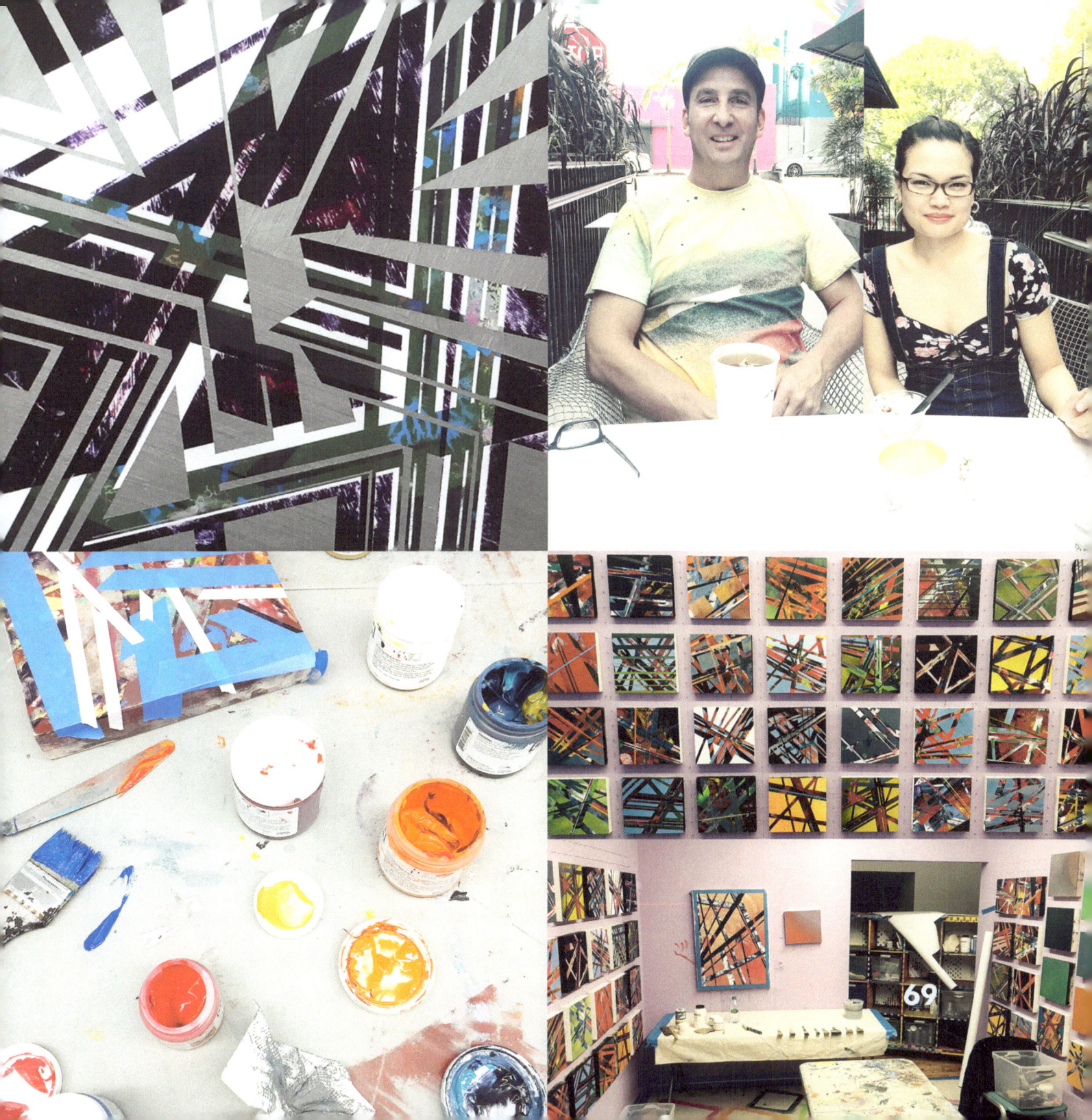

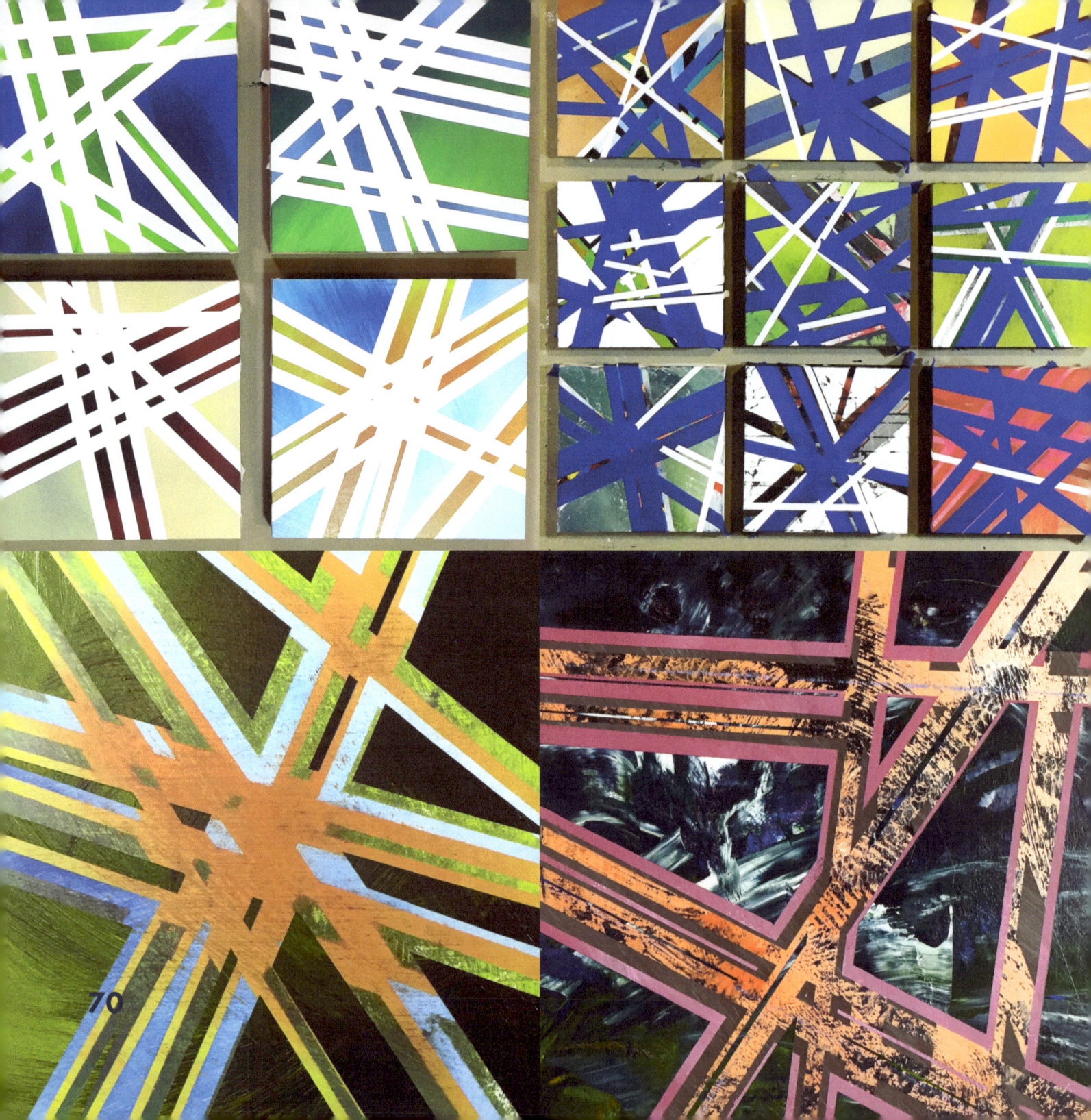

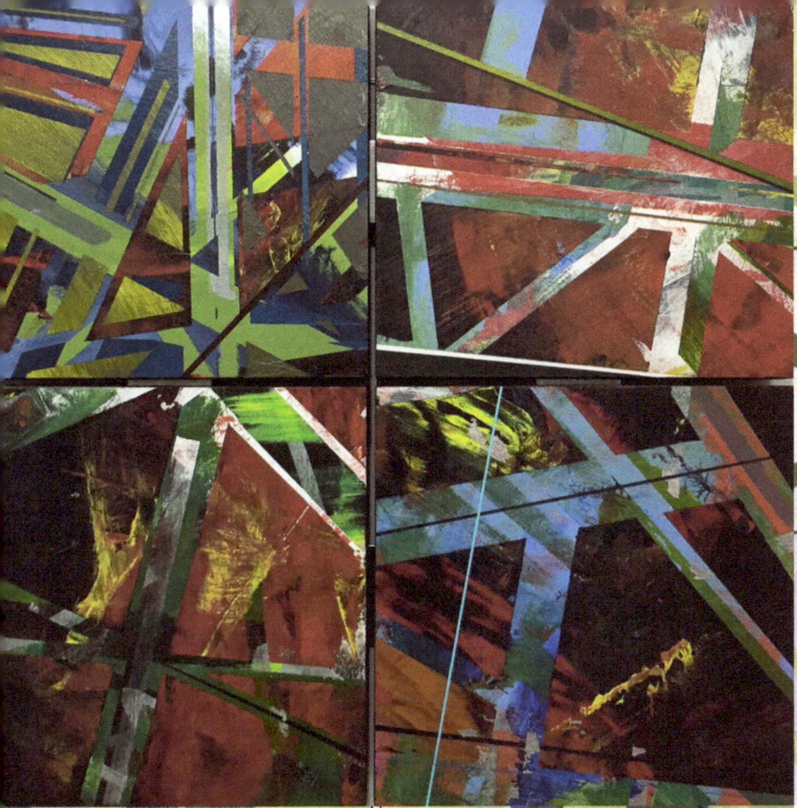

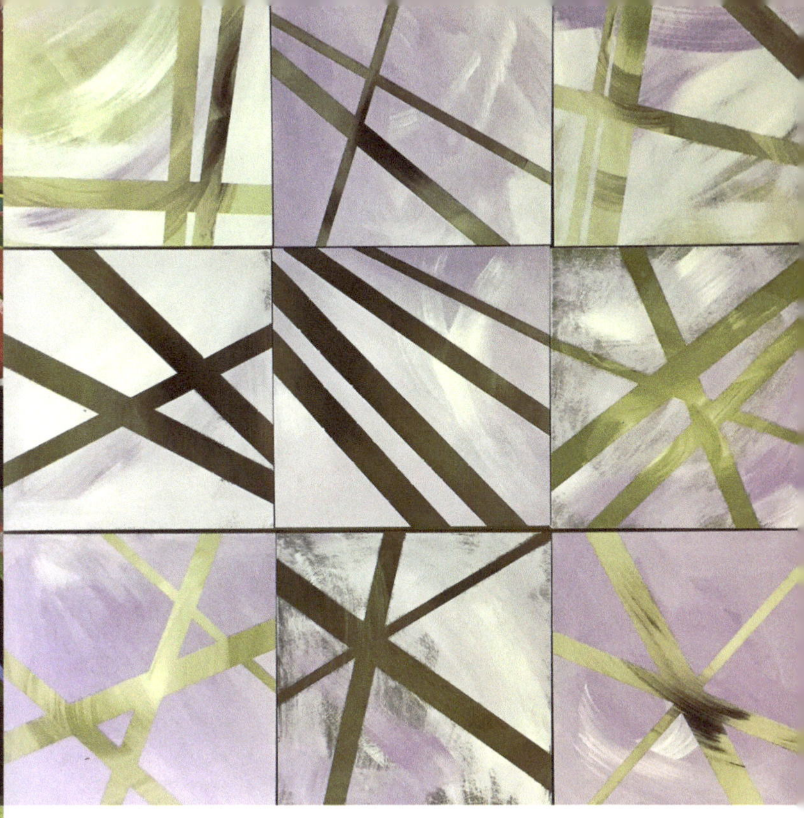

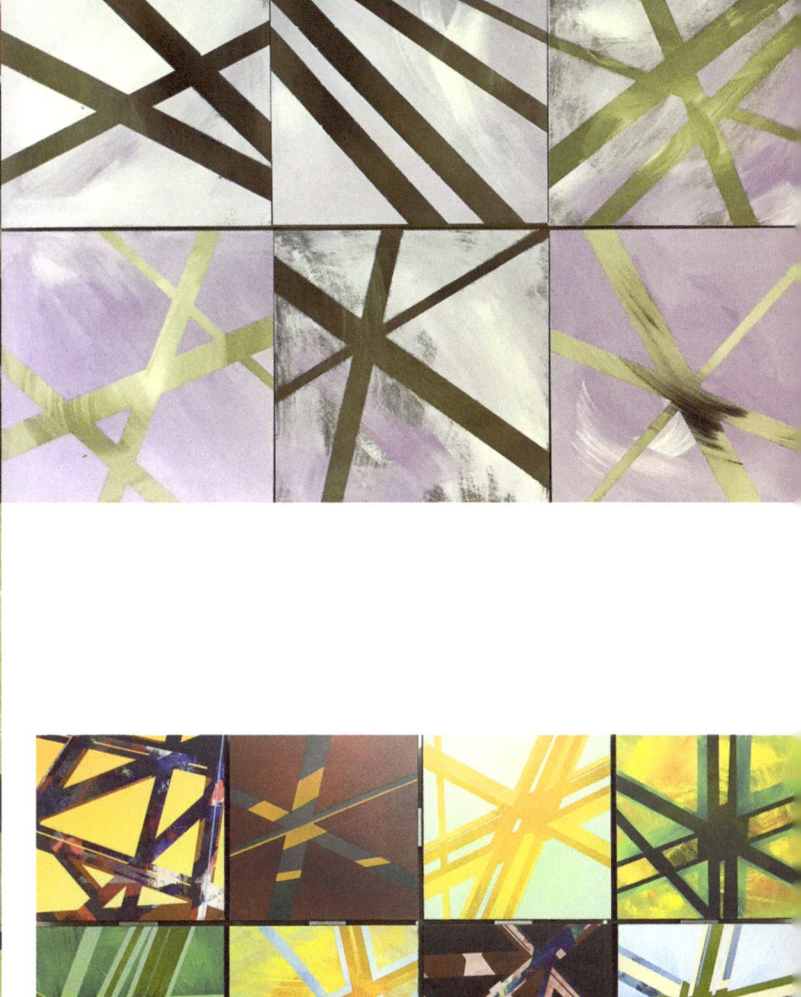

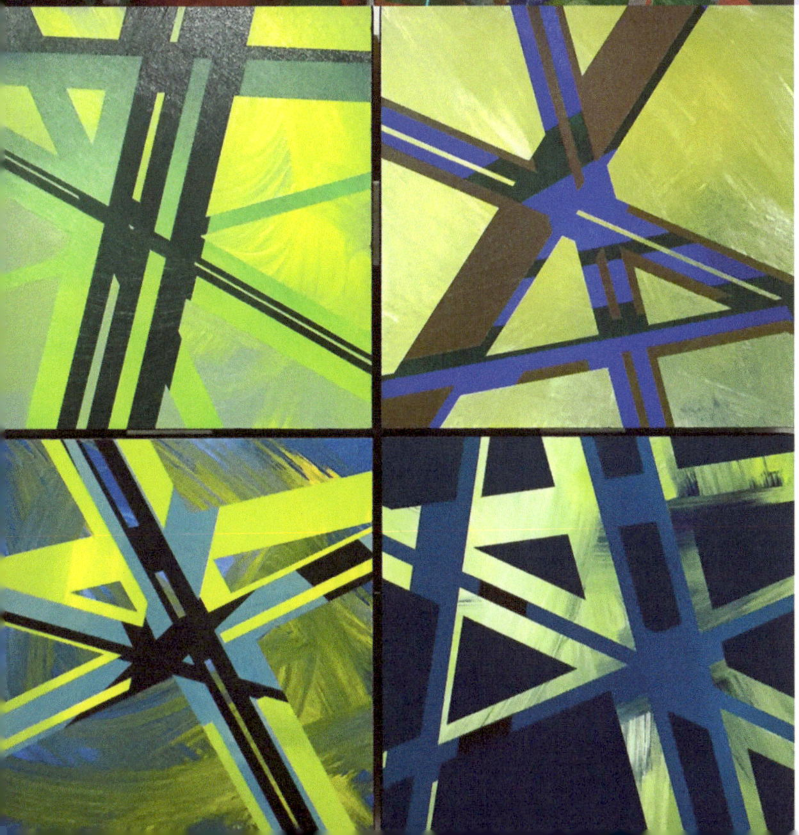

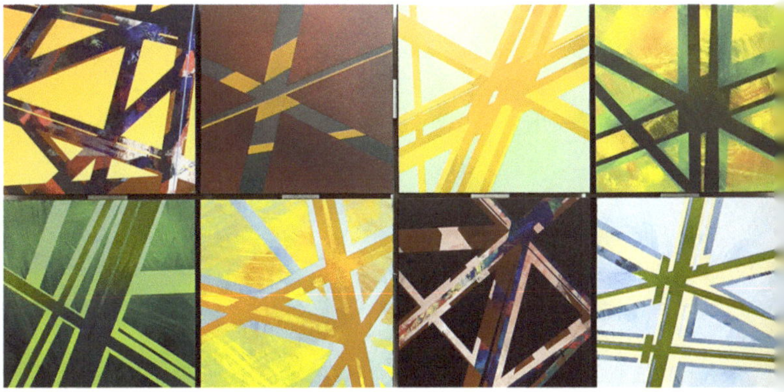

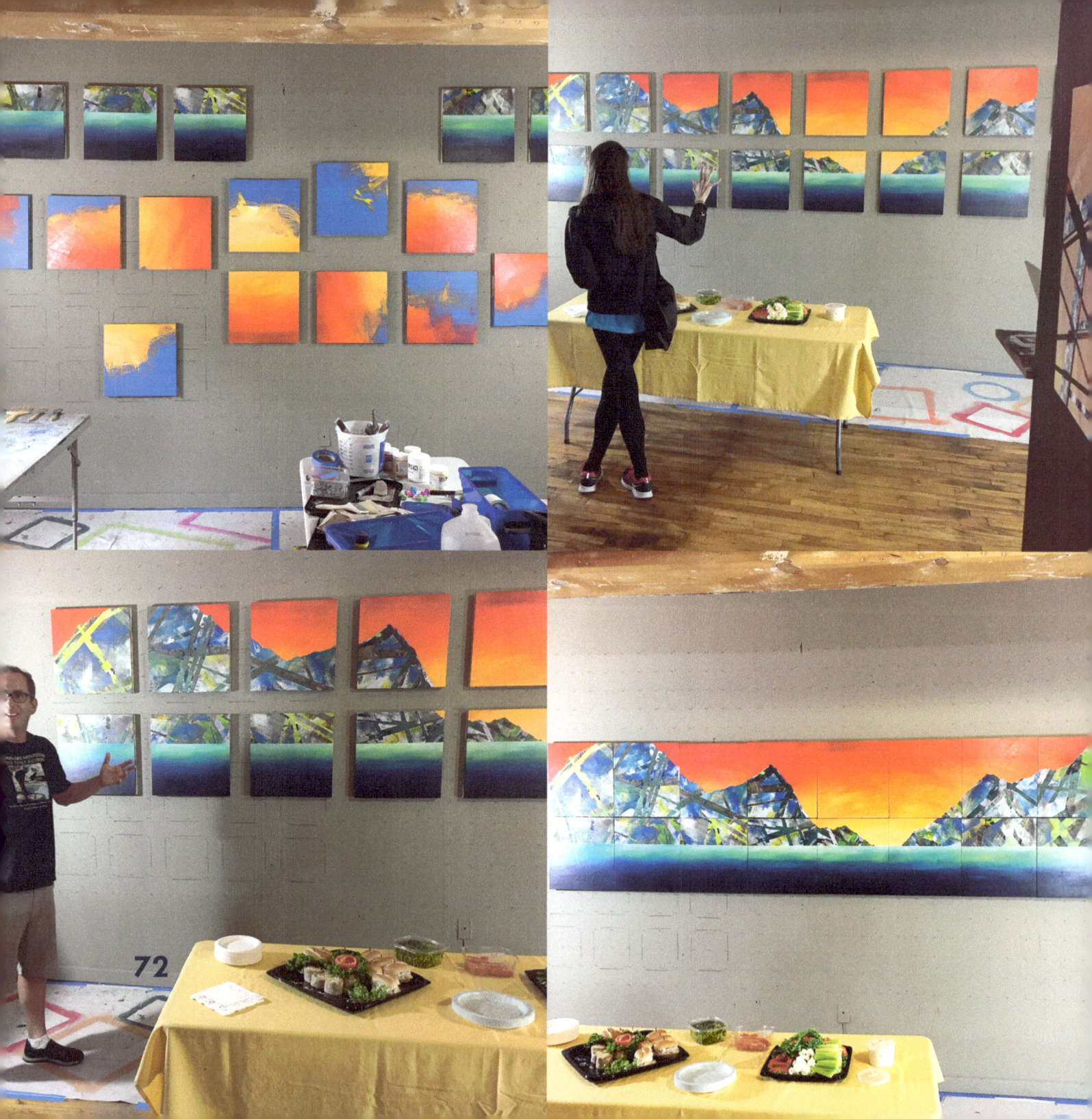

72

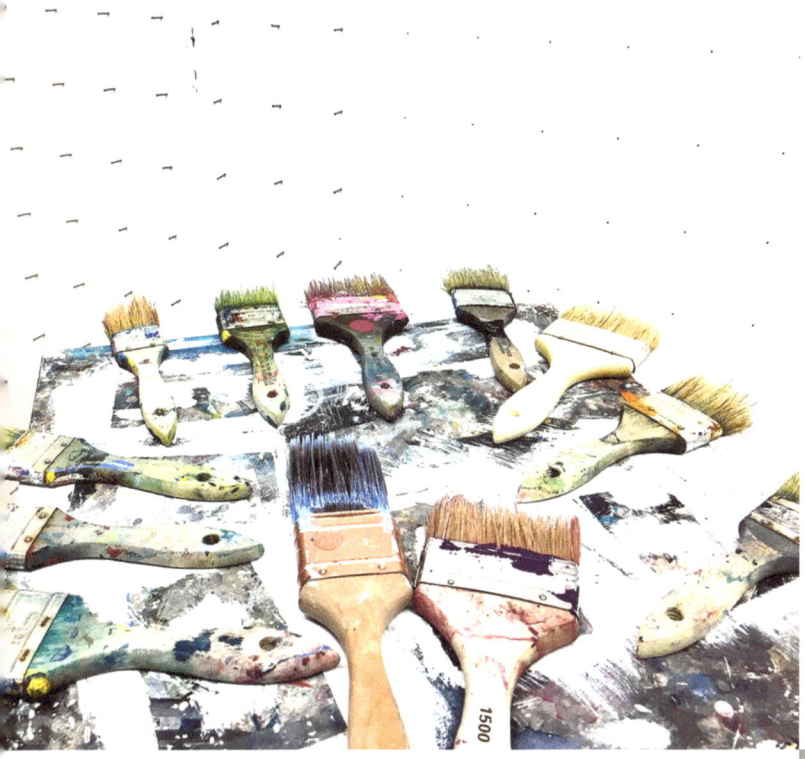

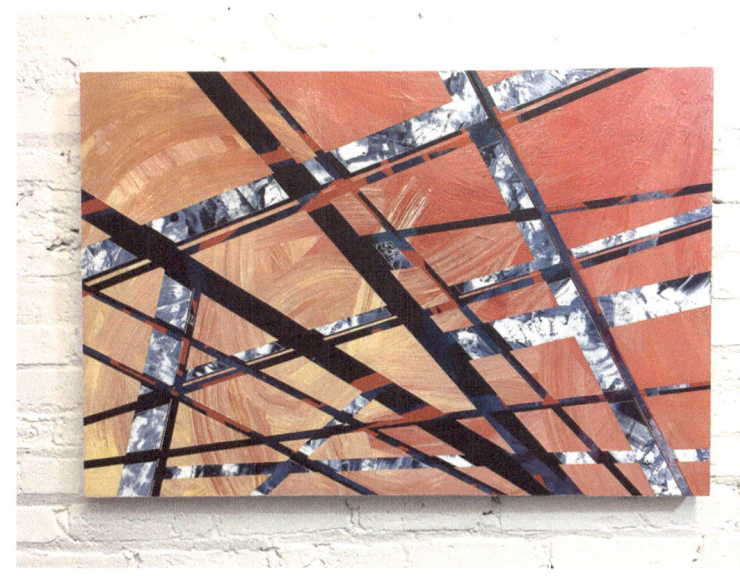

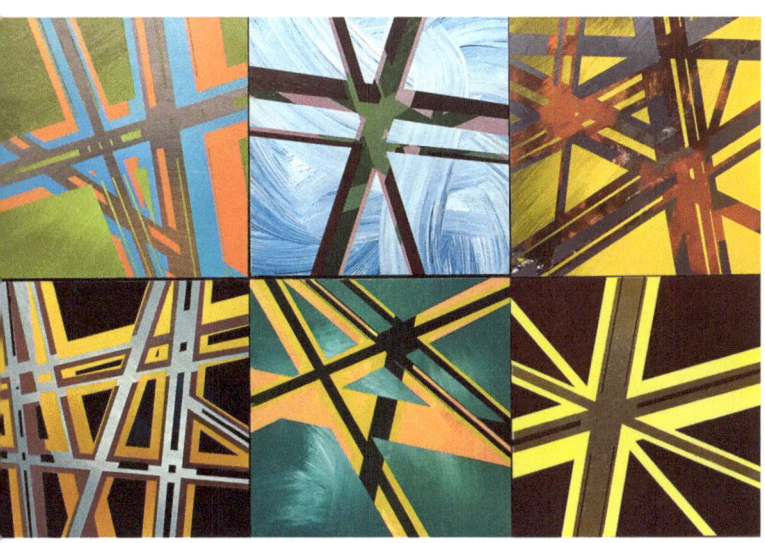

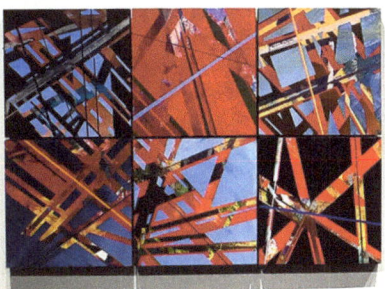

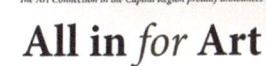

The Art Connection in the Capital Region proudly announces

All in *for* Art
at Landon School

Part of the ACCR Art + Community series

April 17– 28, 2017

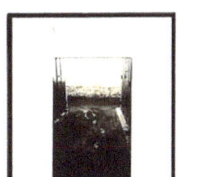

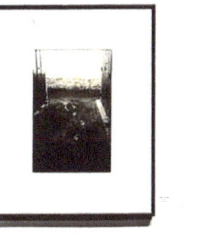

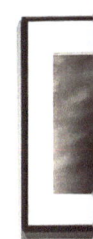

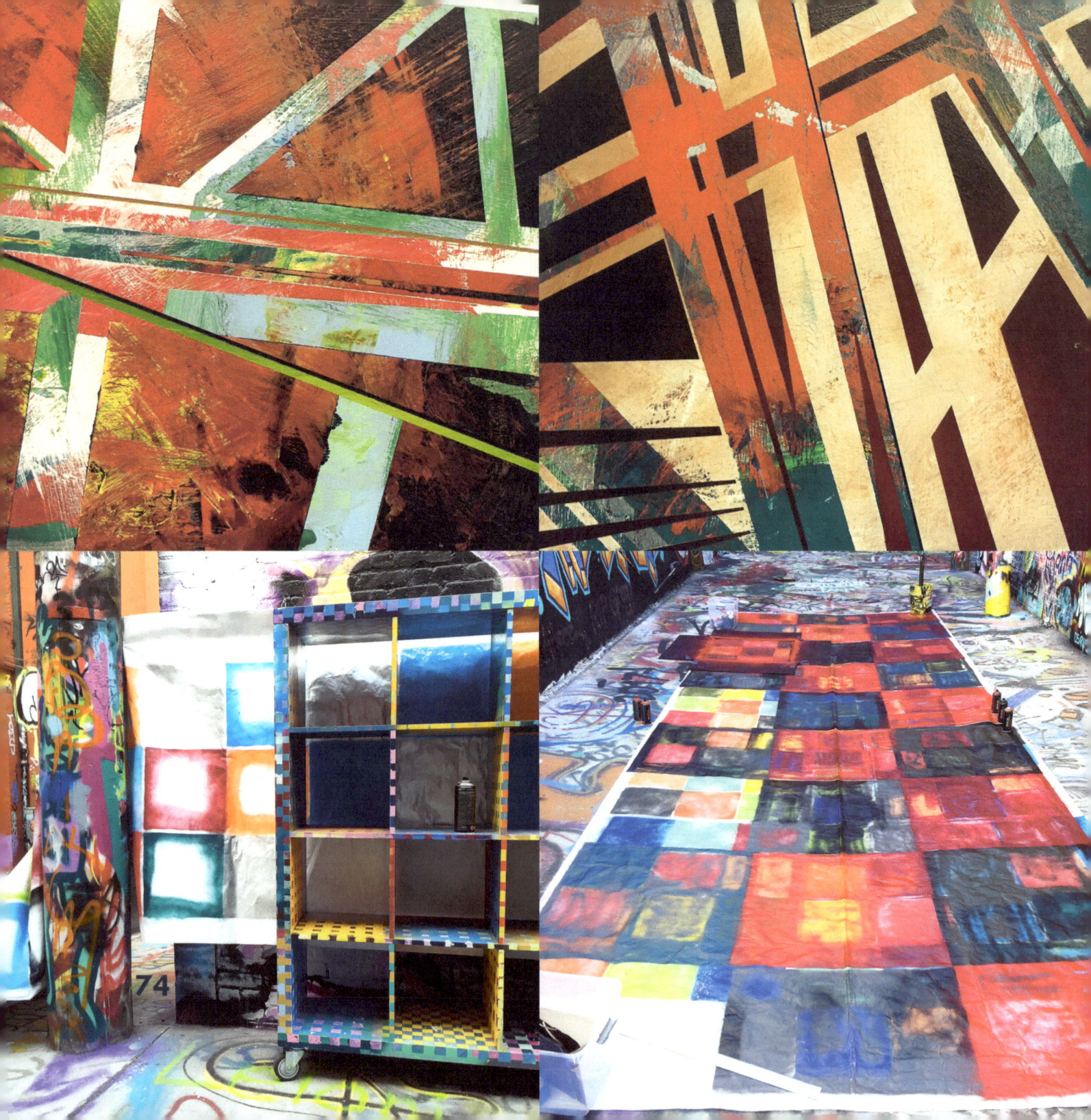

74

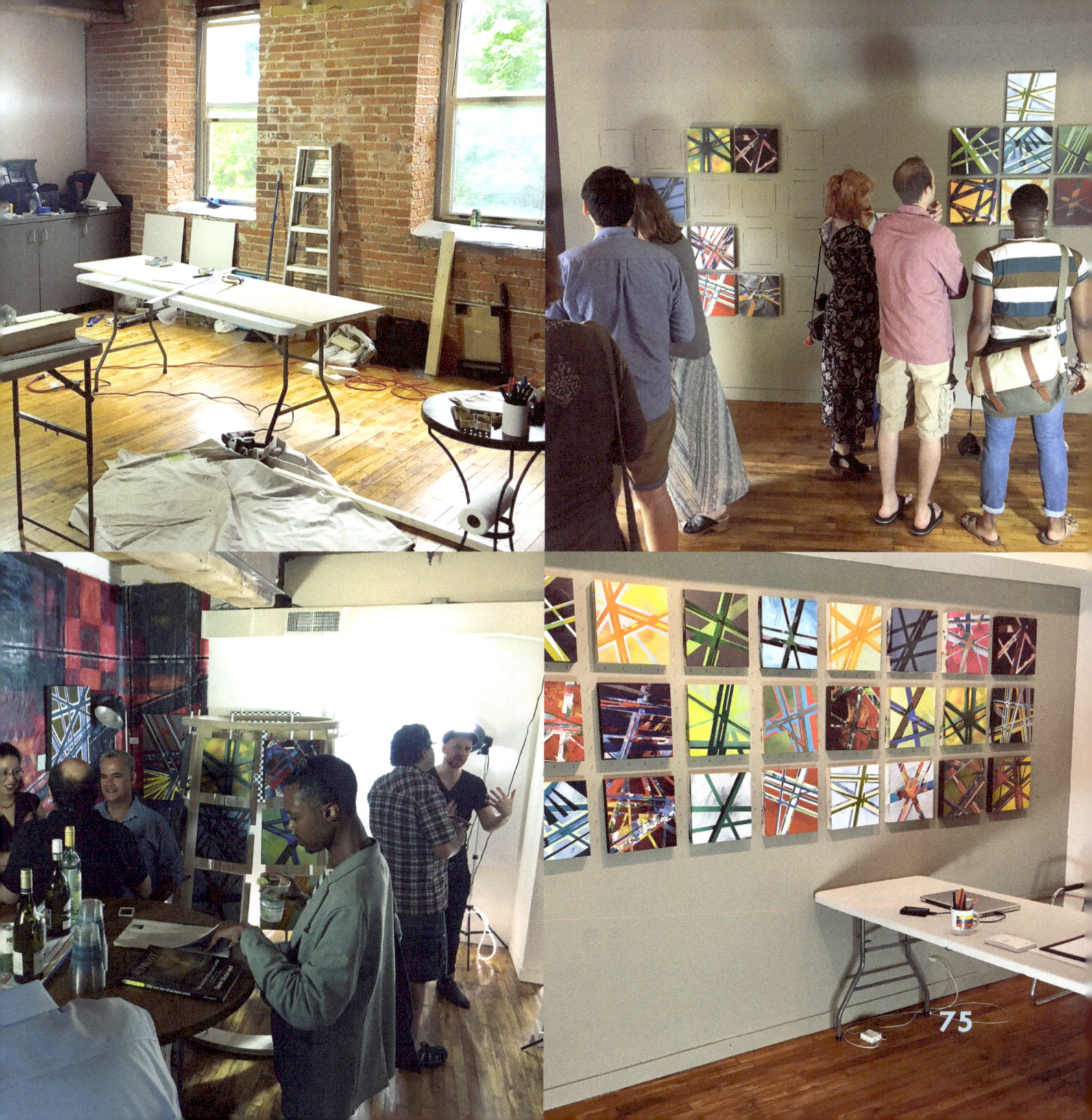

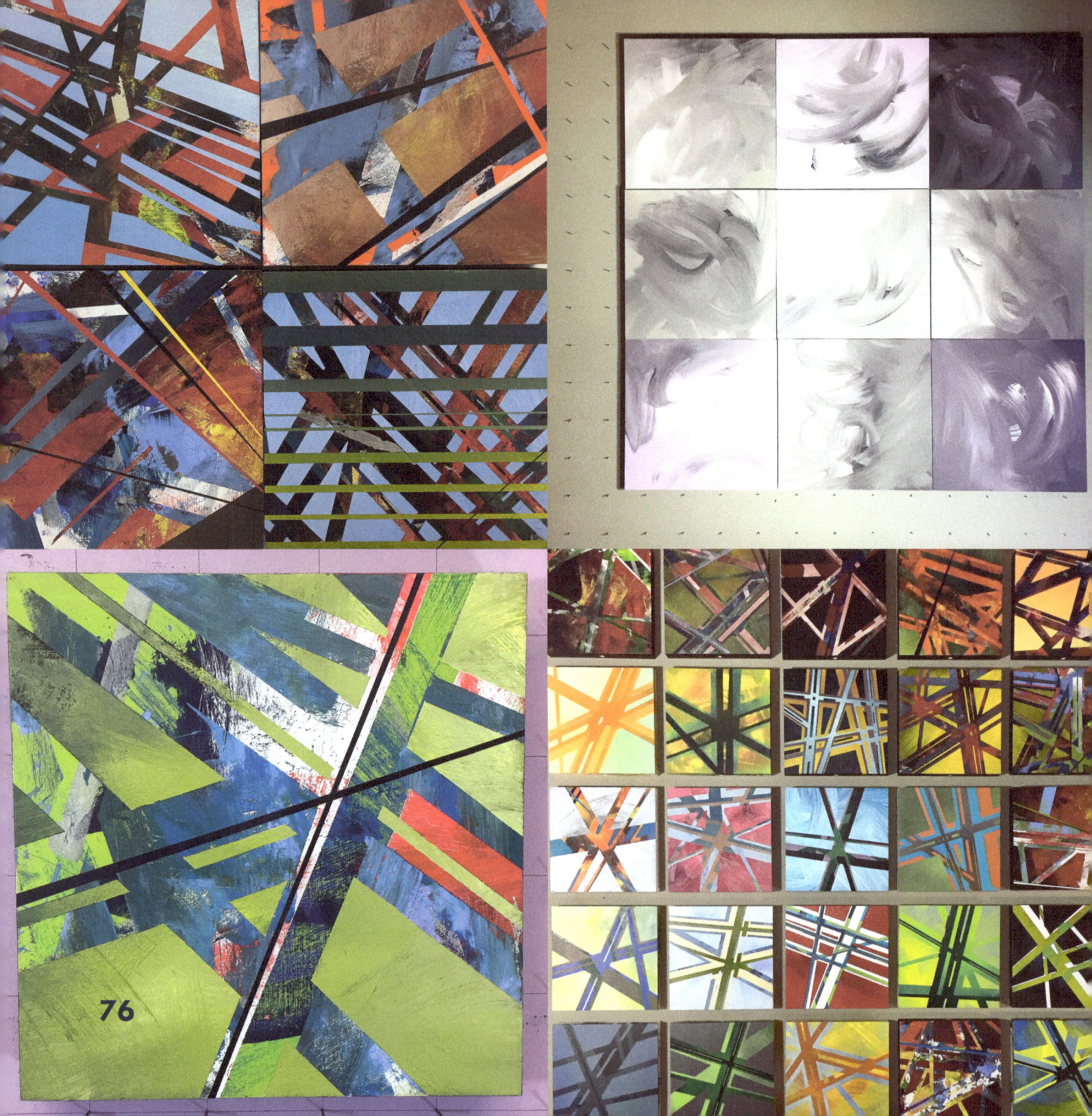

76

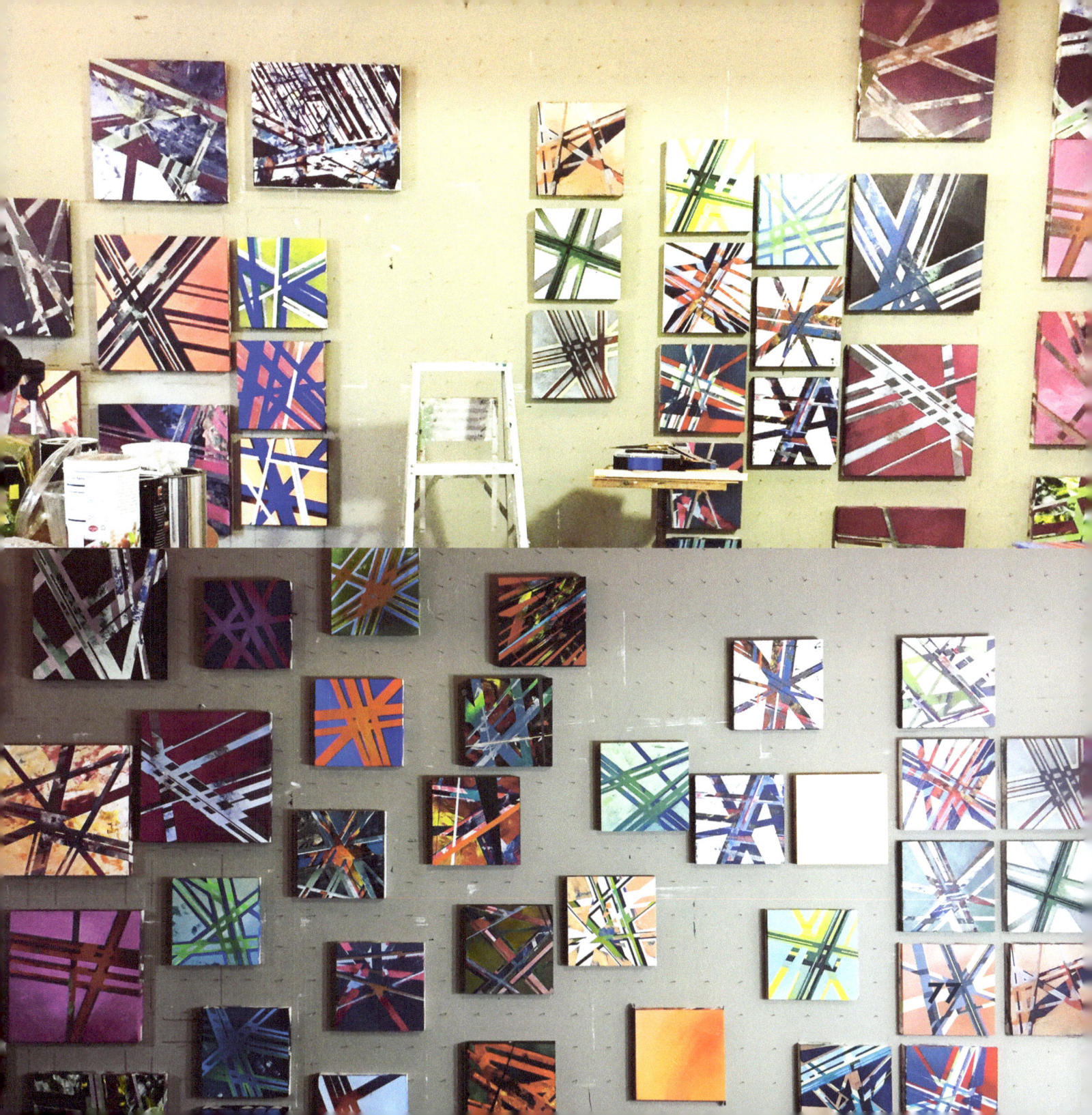

MARSHALL CRAFT ASSOCIATES, ARCHITECTS

78

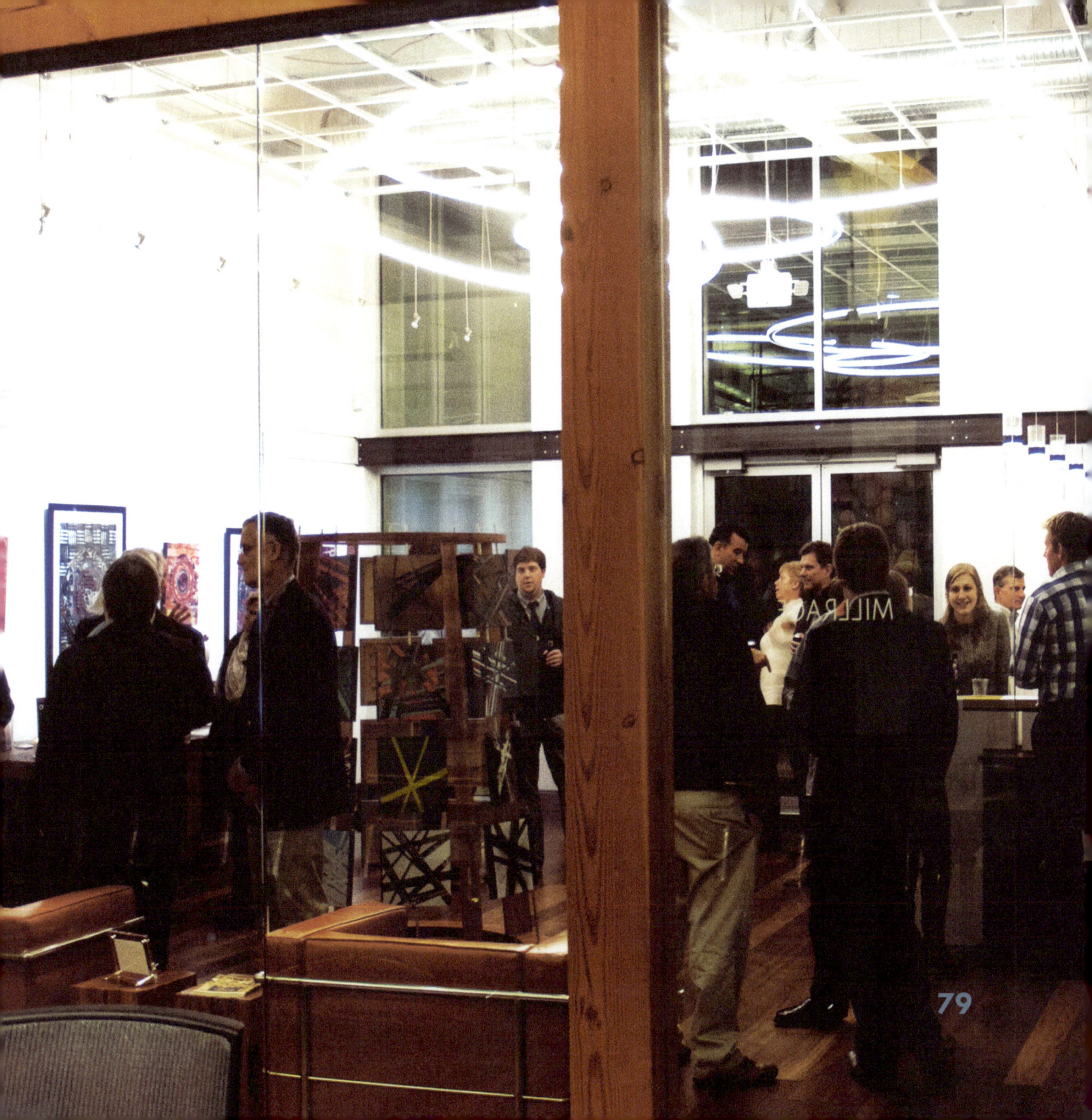

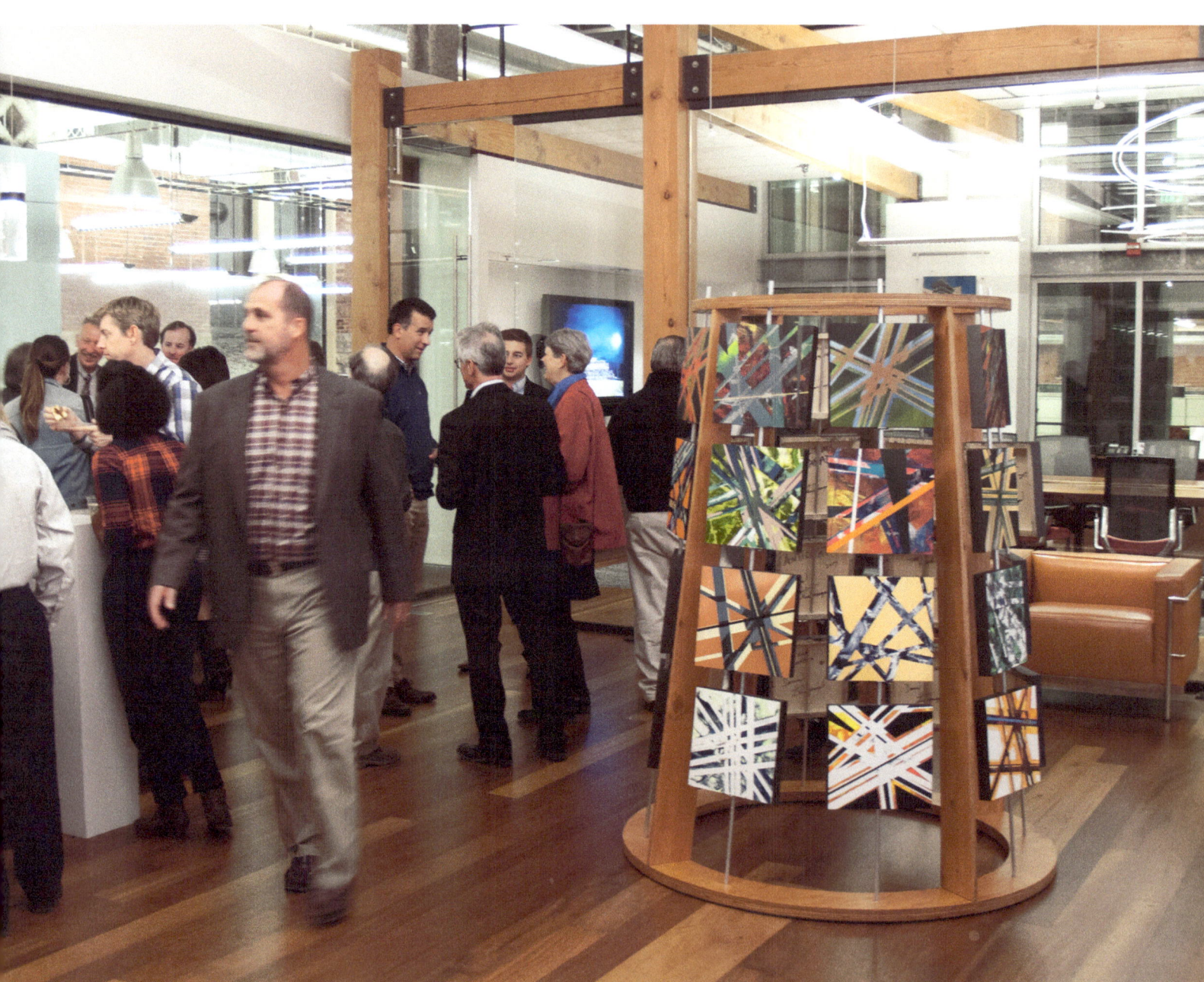

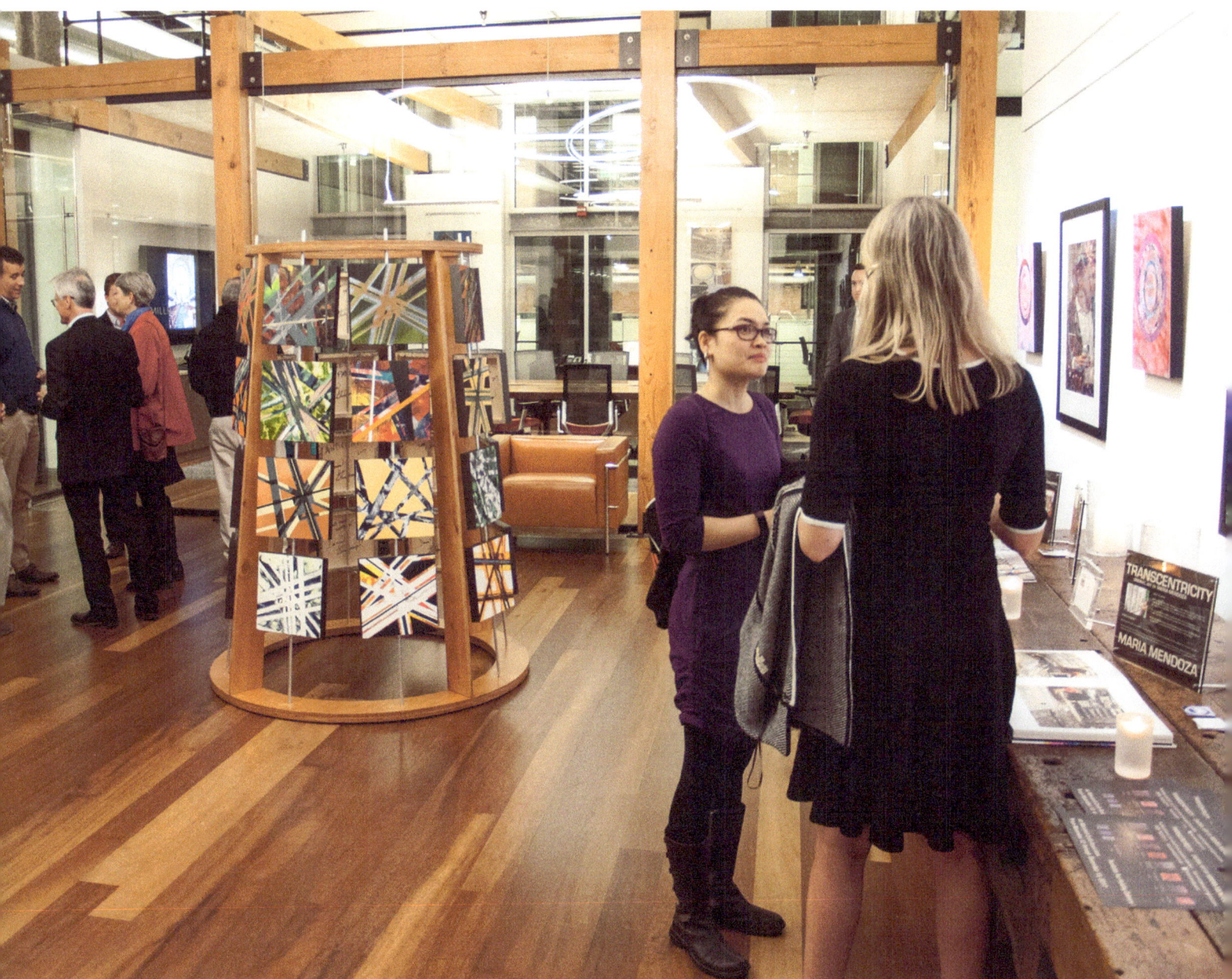

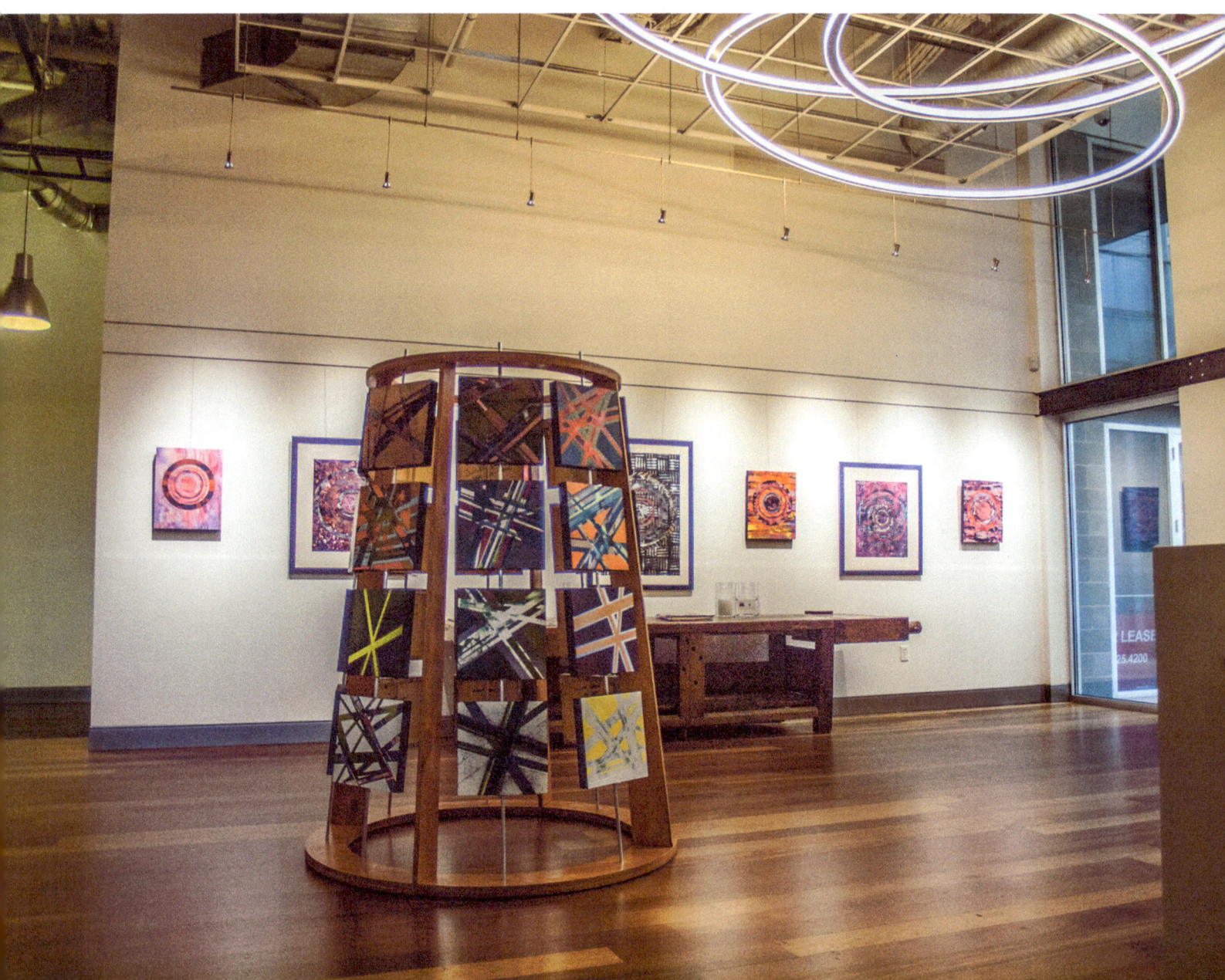

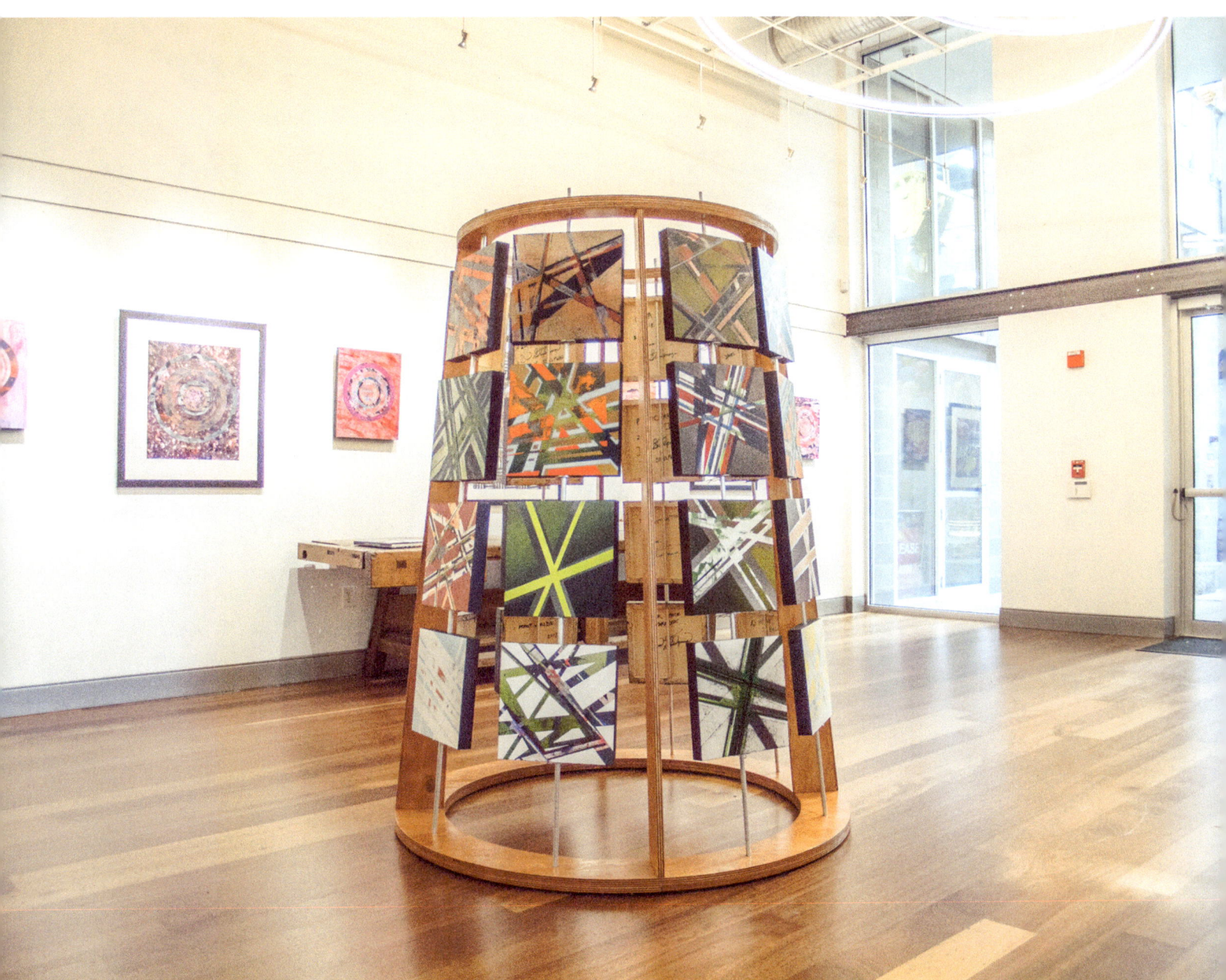

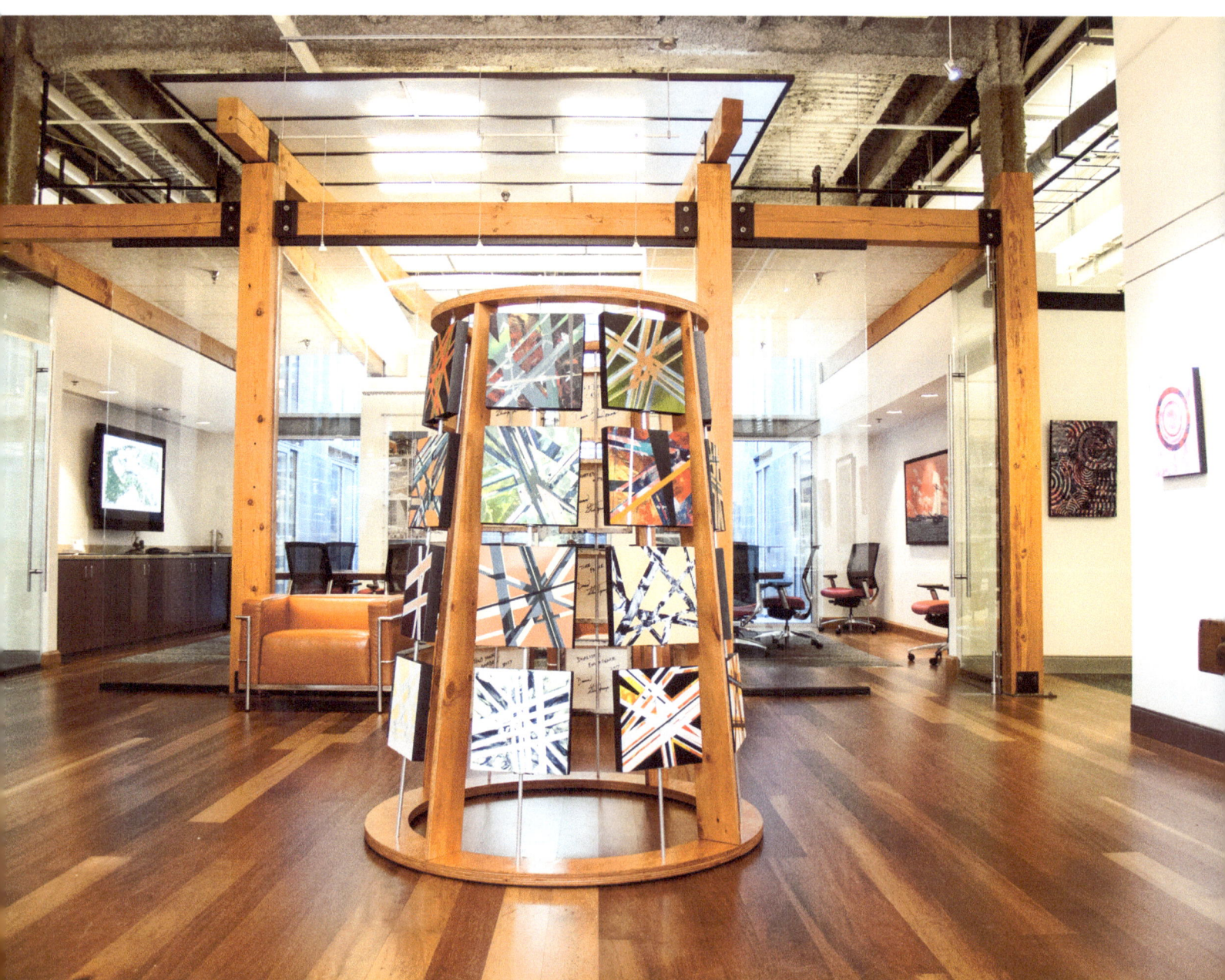

VECTOR SPACE PARADOX

DEDICATED IN LOVING MEMORY OF JOHN CLAY STUELPNAGEL

WITH LOVE AND GRATITUDE TO VIRGINIA L. STUELPNAGEL

LOVE AND THANKS TO MARIA MENDOZA FOR
CREATIVE HELP AND INSPIRATION

COVER PHOTO BY BRENNAN LEE

ADDITIONAL PHOTOS BY MARIA MENDOZA AND ROB GROSSMAN

DISPLAY ASSEMBLY BUILT BY SCOTT PENNINGTON
AND DESIGNED BY DANIEL STUELPNAGEL,
SCOTT PENNINGTON AND MARIA MENDOZA

WITH SPECIAL THANKS TO THE TEDXJHU COMMITTEE AT
JOHNS HOPKINS UNIVERSITY, MARSHALL CRAFT ASSOCIATES ARCHITECTS,
AIA BALTIMORE AND RPI CONSULTANTS

DANIEL STUELPNAGEL

JOHNS HOPKINS UNIVERSITY
TEDXJHU FEATURED ARTIST 2017

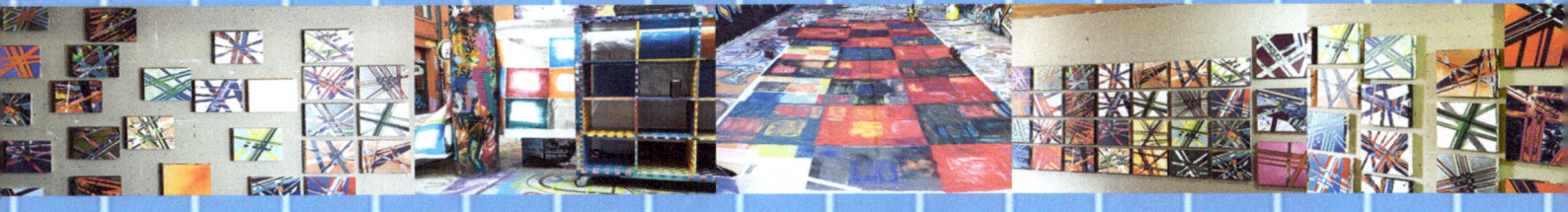

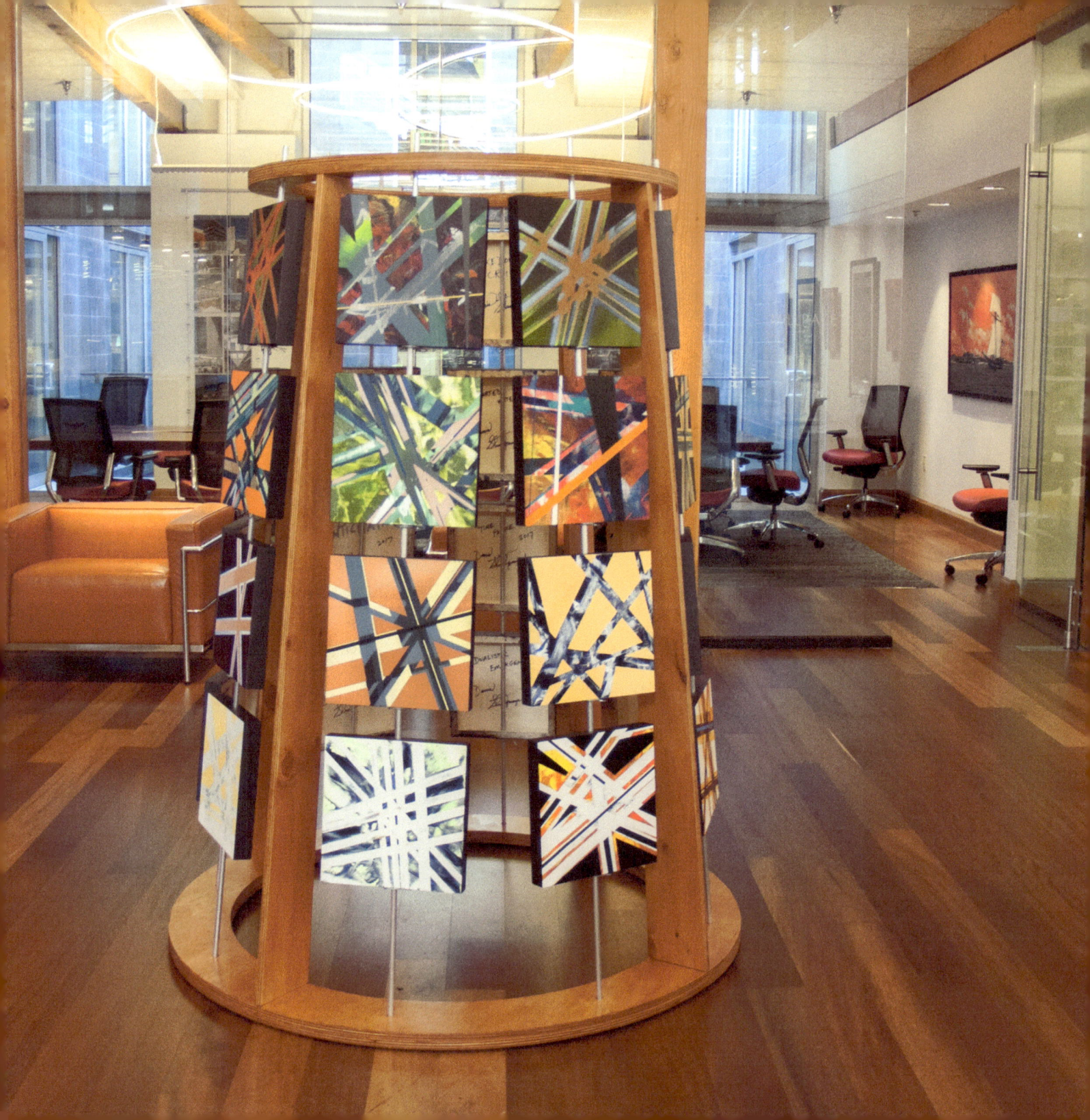